E242
EDUCATION: A SECOND-LEVEL COU

LEARNING FOR ALL

UNIT 8/9
DIFFERENCE AND DISTINCTION

Prepared for the course team by
Will Swann

The Open University

E242 COURSE READERS

There are two course readers associated with E242; they are:

BOOTH, T., SWANN, W., MASTERTON, M. and POTTS, P. (eds) (1992) *Learning for All 1: curricula for diversity in education*, London, Routledge (**Reader 1**).

BOOTH, T., SWANN, W., MASTERTON, M. and POTTS, P. (eds) (1992) *Learning for All 2: policies for diversity in education*, London, Routledge (**Reader 2**).

TELEVISION PROGRAMMES AND AUDIO-CASSETTES

There are eight TV programmes and three audio-cassettes associated with E242. They are closely integrated into the unit texts and there are no separate TV or cassette notes. However, further information about them may be obtained by writing to Open University Educational Enterprises Ltd, 12 Cofferidge Close, Stony Stratford, Milton Keynes MK11 1BY.

Cover illustration shows a detail from 'Midsummer Common' by Dorothy Bordass.

The Open University, Walton Hall, Milton Keynes, MK7 6AA

First published 1992. Reprinted 1994, 1998, 1999

Designed by the Graphic Design Group of The Open University

Typeset by The Open University

Printed in the United Kingdom by Page Bros, Norwich.

ISBN 0 7492 6109 9

This unit forms part of an Open University course; the complete list of units is printed at the end of this book. If you have not enrolled on the course and would like to buy this or other Open University material, please write to Open University Educational Enterprises Ltd, 12 Cofferidge Close, Stony Stratford MK11 1BY, United Kingdom. If you wish to enquire about enrolling as an Open University student, please write to the Admissions Office, The Open University, PO Box 48, Walton Hall, Milton Keynes MK7 6AB, United Kingdom.

1.4

CONTENTS

1 INTRODUCTION

1.1   In Unit 6/7 we discussed the ways in which teachers in mainstream schools have tried to provide learning experiences which take account of, and respond to, the diversity of their classes. We considered examples of lessons in which there were children with a wide range of interests and attainments, including children who have been identified and labelled as having learning difficulties. But you may feel that we have also stepped back a little since Unit 1/2, when we introduced you to the Grove Primary School, which includes many children with disabilities, and to Ravenstonedale School, where Chris Raine, who has Down's syndrome, attends full time. Now we are nearly halfway through the course; what happened to the idea of a *fully* comprehensive school?

1.2   You will know by now some of the many ways in which schools in the United Kingdom are *not* fully comprehensive. As you move through the rest of the course, we shall identify further ways in which the education system does not match this aspiration. To some people, this is a source of regret. To others, it is regrettable that anyone should aspire to such a state of affairs in the first place. But views on who should, and should not, be members of mainstream schools, the terms on which they should take up membership, and whether all are entitled to the same 'membership rights' are not quite as simple as this. The distinctions people wish to make between different groups of pupils are often complex. One person may hold the view that there should be selection at age 11 for grammar schools, support the right of children with disabilities to attend grammar schools, and be a fierce advocate of selection for special schools for children with learning difficulties.

1.3   Debates about selection – what kinds we should have, how it should be done, what effect it has, in whose interests it is done – are never far from the top of the educational agenda. It may be a novel experience for you to think about segregation for separate special education as a form of selection, similar in kind to selection for grammar schools, or for different streams within one school. We can think of attitudes to selection and segregation as varying with regard to:

- the degree of diversity of attainment that can be accommodated in a single group of learners at different ages;

- the degree of diversity of attainment that can be accommodated in a single group of learners in different parts of the curriculum;

- the kinds of differences between pupils that should be marked by attendance at different schools, as against different groups in the same class, or in the same school;

- the way in which teaching methods should adapt to the diversity in the group.

1.4   In thinking about the degree of diversity that can be contained within a single group of learners, we should not assume that people operate simple cut-off points below which they believe children should be excluded. Teachers may be happy to contain children with a wide range of attainments in a single class provided they are not disruptive. Secondary schools may favour the inclusion of children in academic streams who have difficulties in reading, provided they are identified as having a 'specific learning difficulty'. Primary schools may find it easier to include a child with Down's syndrome whose spoken language development is still in the early stages, than a child who is struggling to read and write and has no obvious disability. And many such judgements depend critically on the resources available to support the school and its teachers.

1.5   The combination of principles, practice and constraints produces a great variety of standpoints, from those who pursue an ideal of mainstream schools which include almost all learners in almost all parts of the curriculum, at almost all ages, to those who pursue the contrary ideal of a system which is divided into schools of different kinds for learners of different kinds, in which there are classes which make yet further distinctions between smaller groups of learners. Thus some aim for as much heterogeneity as possible within each group of learners; some for as much homogeneity as possible; and others for various points between. In this unit we are going to investigate how the way we teach children in both mainstream and special schools makes distinctions between different groups of children. We shall examine the kinds of distinctions of experience, in and out of the classroom, that are created, and we shall ask whether and how these distinctions are justified. We shall see that some special arrangements enable learners to be part of heterogeneous groups. Other kinds of special arrangements have the opposite effect; and the effects of yet others are hotly disputed. As with other parts of the course, this unit gives you an opportunity to think through your own views on who should be a member of mainstream schools and what membership rights they should have.

HOW TO STUDY THIS UNIT

1.6   There are five sections following this introduction. All the unit's readings are from Reader 1, *Learning for All 1: curricula for diversity in education*. There are no TV or cassette programmes. Below is a summary of the content of each section, followed by the titles of the reader articles you will be required to read for it.

Section 2 Making and marking distinctions between learners

In Section 2 we discuss the effects of selection for special provision on children's school experience, in the light of the effects of selection within mainstream schools. We ask whether all children share in a common curriculum, and we discuss the impact of the National Curriculum on aspirations for a common curricular entitlement for all children.

' "Totally impractical!": integrating "special care" within a special school' by Jenny Corbett (Reader 1, Chapter 17).

'Hardening the hierarchies: the National Curriculum as a system of classification' by Will Swann (Reader 1, Chapter 7).

Section 3 Access to the mainstream

Section 3 is about ways in which children with physical and sensory disabilities become members of diverse mainstream groups through the use of information technology, through changes in classroom arrangements and through changes in classroom language.

'Expanding horizons: microtechnology and access to the National Curriculum' by Christopher and Rowena Onions (Reader 1, Chapter 14).

'Signing and talking in a Leeds primary school' by Beate Schmidt-Rohlfing (Reader 1, Chapter 13).

Section 4 Preparing for the mainstream: conductive education

Section 4 discusses conductive education, a curriculum for children with physical disabilities that is very different from mainstream curricula. It raises issues about the idea that a special curriculum can *prepare* children for the mainstream curriculum.

'Conductive education: contrasting perspectives' by Mike Oliver and Virginia Beardshaw with an introduction by Will Swann (Reader 1, Chapter 16).

Section 5 Separate and special?

Section 5 concerns learners who present some of the greatest challenges to the notion of a non-selective curriculum. It discusses the ways in which children who are both deaf and blind, and children who have profound learning difficulties, are taught.

'Returning to basics: a curriculum at Harperbury Hospital School' by Dave Hewett and Melanie Nind (Reader 1, Chapter 18).

Section 6 From special to mainstream

Section 6 concludes the unit with a discussion of how one teacher and writer has moved away from a selective approach towards a more non-selective view of how we should respond to the diversity of pupils, and challenges you to consider your own standpoint.

'Becoming a reflective teacher' by Mel Ainscow (Reader 1, Chapter 15).

2 MAKING AND MARKING DISTINCTIONS BETWEEN LEARNERS

2.1   When children become members of a special school, or join a special unit in a mainstream school, or are withdrawn for part of the timetable, they become part of a system of beliefs, practices and relationships which makes up the way of life of the special provision they have joined. They also become subject to a network of beliefs, held by people outside special provision, about what it means to belong to it, and how membership affects one's place in other social groups. Such features of schooling have been called the 'hidden curriculum' but the term does not seem very apposite since some features can be very overt. In this section we shall explore some aspects of what it means for pupils to be selected for separate special provision. What are the effects of selection on these children, and on how they are viewed by teachers and other children?

Activity 1   The consequences of segregation

Note down the changes in a pupil's experience that you think have resulted from (or that you suspect would result from) being placed in some form of special educational provision. These might include changes in:

- the way pupils are taught;

- the way they see themselves and other children;

- the way other children see them;

- their social lives in and out of school;

- their relationships with teachers and their families.

This activity is to prime you for the discussion that follows. At the end of this section, and again at the end of the unit, you might find it useful to compare your list with the issues we take up.

SELECTION AND DIFFERENTIATION IN THE MAINSTREAM

2.2   We need to see the consequences of selection for special provision in the light of the wider system of selection of which it is part. Very few primary schools place children into separate classes based on attainment, but selection within classes is commonplace. There might be language groups, sitting at different tables in the classroom, doing different activities, created on the basis of reading age. For mathematics, children might be in different groups, formed on the basis of different test results. In other schools, groups will not be selected by attainment at all. Selection becomes steadily more apparent as children get older. In some parts of the country children are still selected by ability at 11 or 12 to attend different schools. But selection is also pervasive within most comprehensive secondary schools. Some secondary schools maintain non-selected groups across the curriculum all the way to Year 11, but these are rare. By Year 9 most secondary schools have introduced selection for some or all of the curriculum.

2.3   There are three main ways in which secondary schools select pupils into ability groups. *Streaming* involves dividing a year group into forms which are ordered by attainment; the top stream consists of the 30 or so pupils judged to be most able, the second stream contains the next 30 or so in the ranking, and so on. Streams remain intact for the whole of the curriculum, and often for several years. *Banding* is a modified form of streaming in which children are put into large groups, called bands, on the basis of ability. Each band contains enough children for several classes, and within the band, classes are formed either on a purely random basis, or taking other factors, such as primary school membership, into account. These classes stay together for most or all of the timetable. *Setting* is a form of grouping which attempts to allow for differences in attainment in different subjects. Groups are selected by attainment in separate subjects. In principle pupils can be in a high set in one subject and a low set in another. Secondary schools vary extensively in the way pupils are grouped. Often different departments use different strategies. An English department may not select at all, but the mathematics department in the same school may set pupils throughout their secondary education. It is also common for schools to use different strategies for different year groups. Many secondary schools do not select in Year 7, but begin to do so in Years 8 and 9.

2.4   The effects of selection within mainstream schools have been widely studied and debated in the past 25 years. Stephen Ball (1981) studied the selection processes in one comprehensive school which he called Beachside. Over three years the school moved from a system of banding to mixed ability grouping in Years 7, 8 and 9. Under the original system, there were three bands. Bands 1 and 2 each had four parallel forms. Band 3 had two ability-grouped forms, one of which was called 'remedial'. Children were placed in bands on the basis of reports and recommendations from primary schools, based in some cases on test results. This system of grouping had enormous consequences for the experiences of both teachers and pupils. Ball argued that banding gave rise to stereotypes of pupils held by the teachers at Beachside. He presented 'composite band-profiles, constructed from teachers' descriptions':

The band 1 child

Has academic potential … will do O-levels … and a good number will stay on to the sixth form … likes doing projects … knows what the teacher wants … is bright, alert and enthusiastic … can concentrate … produces neat work … is interested … wants to get on … is grammar school material … you can have discussions with … friendly … rewarding … has common sense.

The band 2 pupil

Is not interested in school work ... difficult to control ... rowdy and lazy ... has little self control ... is immature ... loses and forgets books with monotonous regularity ... cannot take part in discussions ... is moody ... of low standard ... technical inability ... lacks concentration ... is poorly behaved ... not up to much academically.

The band 3 child

Is unfortunate ... is low ability ... maladjusted ... anti-school ... lacks a mature view of education ... mentally retarded ... emotionally unstable and ... a waste of time.

(Ball, 1981, pp. 38–9)

2.5   A stereotype is a set of beliefs about the members of a group, ascribed on the basis of group membership, rather than personal characteristics. Ball argues that pupils were dealt with not according to their individual characters and attainments, but according to the band stereotypes that had evolved within the school. These stereotypes acted as filters through which pupils were perceived, and were part of a set of identities and expectations created by the banding system which fostered negative attitudes and disruptive behaviour amongst band 2 pupils:

> [The] estimated potential of ... pupils based on the reports from their junior schools, which led to their being allocated to band 2, was such as to label them 'failures' in a system that had not given them the opportunity to show their worth ... This system required them to respect it and to accept from it values which stressed the importance of hard work, enthusiasm, good behaviour and academic striving – even though, by assigning them to band 2, the system had assumed and accepted that they would be lacking in these qualities. Whereas it was suggested to the children that they were placed in band 2 so that they could be given work more suited to their abilities, what actually happened ... was that the teachers simply expected them to be pupils of low, second-rate ability. As one Human Studies teacher put it, 'Band 2 lessons are essentially dull for both teacher and pupils.' For these children, their secondary school careers had begun with a decision which meant that they were to strive for rewards in a race from which they had already been disqualified. But despite this they were to try their hardest to run as fast as the winners, and expect to be punished if they did not keep to the rules.
>
> (Ball, 1981, pp. 39–40)

2.6   There is an immediate objection to this account. The teachers' beliefs about the bands may have been based on the evidence of pupils' behaviour, and so may have been a result rather than a cause of the problems. In fact band 2 had a higher level of detentions and absences in Years 8 and 9 than band 1. There are at least two replies to this objection.

First, in the primary schools the attainments of pupils later assigned to band 1 and band 2 overlapped. Some children in band 2 left junior school with higher scores in reading and mathematics tests than some children in band 1 (Ball does not give test scores for band 3). Second, teachers were aware that band 2 pupils were not generally troublesome at the start of their secondary school careers:

> In the first year they started off fresh and the same, but by the end of the first year they began to realize that being in band 2 or band 3 is not quite the same. And in the second year they click and in the third year they switch off; it's tragic.
>
> (Assistant year tutor)
>
> I had a band 2 form in the first and second year, they were tremendously self-motivated, really great kids, there was none of this 'we're at the bottom sod it' in the first year, it really came out in the third.
>
> (Art teacher)
>
> (Ball, 1981, p. 47)

2.7 So in Beachside Comprehensive, selection and grouping encouraged teachers to respond to children according to group identities, associated with different statuses within the school. Selection affected all pupils, and was associated with widely divergent school experiences for different groups. Ball does not claim that children simply conformed to the stereotypes of their teachers, nor that teachers treated children consistently according to band stereotypes. The process is more complex than that.

2.8 The removal of bands did not eliminate the stereotyping. When Beachside moved to mixed ability teaching, the classification of children by attainment did not disappear. It emerged in different ways. Teachers did not stop evaluating pupils in terms of their attainment just because they happened to be in mixed ability groups, nor did they stop communicating these evaluations to pupils. Some teachers grouped by attainment within classes. Teachers' actions often signalled to pupils the differences between them:

> Put up your hands those of you who have started section C on the workcard.
>
> (History teacher)
>
> If you want to read the part of Green you have to be a good fast reader because if you're a slow reader we will be hanging about for you, it's a big part. Put up your hands then if you want to read Green.
>
> (English teacher)
>
> (Ball, 1981, pp. 271, 272)

So the origins of the band stereotypes went deeper than the system of banding. Mixed ability grouping removed from the teachers the opportunity to take their understandings of pupils from band membership. But it did not fundamentally alter the way in which teachers classified children. Instead, mixed ability teaching required teachers to make those classifications from the evidence of pupil performance and individual reputation.

2.9 The separation and ranking of children in school have been referred to as 'differentiation'. This term was used by David Hargreaves (1967) and Colin Lacey (1970) to describe the way in which pupils in the secondary schools they studied came to be categorized and evaluated in terms of their membership of selected groups. Recently, the term 'differentiation' has appeared in many official documents and articles on the curriculum, but in an apparently different guise. In its main guidance document on the National Curriculum and special educational needs, the National Curriculum Council (NCC) said that:

> In both ordinary and special schools good practice is most likely to be advanced when all members of staff are committed to the same aims: providing a broad, balanced, relevant and differentiated curriculum.
>
> (NCC, 1989, p. 3)

In the late 1980s 'differentiation' came to be seen by many learning support teachers as one of their main goals in teaching. Is this the same sort of differentiation that held sway in Beachside Comprehensive? We shall return to this question later in this section and again in the last section of the unit.

SPECIAL PROVISION AND SOCIAL IDENTITY

2.10 We have seen how selection is associated with distinctions between the school experience of different groups of pupils, and how it contributes to the creation of pupil identities in a mainstream setting. Now let's turn to selection for special provision. We shall do this in three stages. First, we examine how special provision is associated with distinctions between the school experience of different groups. Second, we look at the relationship between segregation and stereotyping. Finally, we consider how segregation and stereotyping can work *within* special provision.

Distinctions of treatment

2.11 Special provision can involve distinctions in the way groups of pupils are treated, not all of which are planned by their teachers, and not all of which are desirable. One of the arguments against traditional remedial education concerned the restricted curriculum provided for remedial groups. Another was that pupils were subject to low expectations. These are long standing criticisms of several forms of special provision. One important source of evidence is a series of inspections by Her Majesty's Inspectors of Schools (HMI), carried out in the late 1980s. On the curriculum for pupils with physical disabilities HMI claimed of special schools' curricula:

> Generally ... the situation was not satisfactory. Schools had difficulty in providing the range of subjects and educational experiences necessary to meet pupils' needs; subjects such as science and craft, design and technology (CDT) were generally poorly covered or omitted altogether. The more severe and complex the handicapping condition, the more limited was pupils' access to an appropriate curriculum.
>
> (DES, 1989a, pp. 4–5)

In ordinary schools too, children with physical disabilities sometimes had a limited curriculum. Here the problem was dovetailing pupils' classroom work with various therapies: 'As a result, the balance of providing for pupils' special needs while maintaining breadth and continuity of educational provision was difficult to achieve' (DES, 1989a, p. 5).

2.12   By comparison with these modest criticisms, HMI's views on the curriculum in special schools and units for pupils identified as having 'emotional and behavioural disorders' were unusually strong. In a highly critical review they found deficiencies in accommodation, equipment, organization and teaching approaches:

> ... it was generally the case that ineffective curricular planning was mirrored in poor teaching and learning.
>
> The curriculum on offer was frequently too narrow and lacking in balance. Too much emphasis was often placed on narrowly conceived programmes of work in language and mathematics, with little opportunity for pupils systematically to practise language or number skills in practical situations or in their work in other areas of the curriculum ...
>
> In many cases the curriculum showed major gaps in the range of subjects offered. Most frequently these were in the areas of science, religious and moral education, humanities and the creative arts. In some cases practical subjects received too little attention.
>
> (DES, 1989b, p. 9)

2.13   Such problems are not always the most significant for pupils. Apparently minor distinctions can have a large impact on their lives in school, and yet seem so ordinary as scarcely to be noticed. Some time ago one of us visited a special school for children with physical disabilities to join a discussion group of secondary aged pupils. A teacher asked the group to introduce themselves by giving their names, and then she asked them to say what their disability was. The voices span round the circle: 'spina bifida', 'muscular dystrophy', 'muscular dystrophy', 'cerebral palsy', 'spina bifida' ... This marking of their disabilities as an important personal characteristic was striking. These pupils may have had other things to say about themselves in preference.

2.14   There are many ways in which placement in special provision can serve to foster a distinct group identity. David Cropp (1987) described the objections raised by one group of pupils in the special education unit of a comprehensive school to their 'special' treatment. These pupils took the initiative to complain about a number of distinctions made between themselves and others:

- All forms in the school were named by the year followed by the form teacher's initials, except unit forms, which were titled as 1G, 2G etc.

- Unit pupils were not subject to the same system of sanctions as the rest of the school. Sanctions were either not handed out at all, or were less severe than for other pupils.

- Unit pupils were not required to wear school uniform.

- There was a 'help-link' system in operation in which Year 11 mainstream pupils spent some time with unit pupils, either helping them round the school or with their class work.

- Unit pupils travelled to school in taxis, whereas other pupils travelled on foot or by bus.

- Mainstream pupils received school reports in open envelopes and so could read them before taking them home. Unit pupils were given theirs in sealed envelopes.

- There were a number of differences between the unit pupils' movement about the school and others'. Unit pupils were not allowed to leave the site without an escort, and went early to lunch to avoid the main school rush.

2.15   The pupils in the unit found these distinctions objectionable for two kinds of reasons. They supported their identification as a separate group in the school, and they implied a dependent status as a group of pupils who needed 'help' from others, who were less accountable for their own actions, who were unable to judge for themselves whether they could read their reports and whether they would be safe outside school.

Stereotypes and separation

2.16   From early on, children will produce stereotyped responses towards people with disabilities and learning difficulties if they are invited to. Dominic Abrams and his colleagues (1990) examined the way in which children in Years 5 and 6 in one junior school understood the differences between themselves and children labelled 'mentally handicapped', 'physically handicapped' and 'divvy' (the common term in this school for children with learning difficulties). Their method invited children to respond to the label, rather than to individual children. They asked children to rate these labels on a scale of 1 to 7 on dimensions such as 'knows a lot/not very much' and 'able/unable to feed and dress self'. All the children knew was the name of the fictional child and the label. Children made very few distinctions between the three labels. Labelled children were seen as a homogeneous group, knowing less than normal children, as more likely to do stupid things, to walk funny, not to act properly, to act like a younger child. But these negative views did not affect children's judgements of how labelled children would be treated. They believed that people would be as nice to labelled children as to others, would look after them as well, and would not make fun of them any more than non-labelled children.

2.17   Where do such stereotypes of children with disabilities and learning difficulties come from? Are they supported by separation into special provision? We saw in Unit 6/7 that separate remedial education identified some children as a distinct, devalued and stigmatized group, subject to negative responses from their peers. But this is by no means the only factor at work. We have already seen that in school pupils soon become aware of their place and the place of others in their school's hierarchies of esteem. Children's understanding of disability and difficulties in learning is shaped by many factors: parents and teachers, media images, other pupils' attitudes, personal contact, and so on. All these forces make up the backdrop against which children's understandings of what it means to be in special provision are formed.

2.18   Against this background, how might separation into special provision affect the formation of stereotypes? In Cassette Programme 2 we saw some of the consequences of special school placement for children's attitudes. In one discussion, Bobby, from the junior school, recorded her initial dismay at the thought that she would be joined by children from Sutton, the special school:

> When I first heard that the Sutton School's coming ... 'cos they haven't got a very good reputation if you know what I mean, we thought 'Oh no!' ... 'cos we've heard a lot of things about the Sutton School and we thought 'Oh no, working with the Sutton School.'

Bobby's initial judgements were influenced by the special school's reputation. Membership of the special school appeared to exert an independent and negative impact on her perceptions. Segregation limits the opportunities for children to learn about each others' personal characteristics. Under these conditions stereotyping is a readily available strategy.

2.19   Children in mainstream schools may also seek to make sense of segregation for themselves. Going to a special school is an unusual event that needs explaining, and the conclusions that children reach can be said to form part of the stereotype of a segregated pupil. Stephanie Ince, Heather Johnstone and Will Swann (1985) discussed the views of a small group of children who had moved from a special school for children with a range of disabilities into a local comprehensive school. One of the group, by then attending the comprehensive, reflected on a visit to his old school:

> I find I'm treating them as if they're a bit peculiar. They don't do the same work that we do – it's all easy. You begin to realize what other people think when they see kids at a school like this – they think there must be something wrong.

2.20   Teachers too may need to explain a child's segregated status. In his study of Beachside Comprehensive, Stephen Ball hints that the stereotypes that teachers held of the remedial stream were of a different order to band 2 pupils: 'The misbehaviour of the band 3 pupils tended to be defined in terms of emotional problems or maladjustment, rather than belligerence' (Ball, 1981, p. 23). The behaviour of band 3 pupils was seen by some teachers as beyond the pupils' own control, and indicative of personal pathology. The pupils in band 2 appeared to be held responsible for actions which they had chosen to engage in. Band 3 pupils were judged less able to do anything about their poor performance and behaviour.

2.21   As children pass from mainstream to special provision their difficulties are more likely to be seen as beyond their own control and so calling for different treatment. Brenda Gamble and Judith Palmer (1989) studied attitudes amongst mainstream staff towards children in a primary 'adjustment unit'. This unit, based in a mainstream primary school, was attended by children moved from other schools as a result of 'behavioural and social problems'. Some staff tended to see bad behaviour as requiring responses they might propose for any child:

> Their mothers should give them a good smack.

> They need a clip round the ear! Why should they get away with things other children are punished for?

> (Gamble and Palmer, 1989, pp. 155, 151)

But other members of staff took the view that these children should be treated more cautiously than others:

> I wish I could do something to help them, but I feel that I have insufficient knowledge and that I could upset the behaviour programme. I feel inadequate when I see them misbehave – should I become involved or not? If not, am I doing damage, and vice versa?

> (Gamble and Palmer, 1989, p. 151)

The view that children are not responsible for their conduct can be a concession. But it can also be oppressive, for it means that the child is no longer seen as able to choose one action or another, and it entails the need for other people to control the child's actions.

2.22   Children who see themselves as members of devalued groups face the problems of explaining their social position to themselves and to others and managing its consequences. Most people seek to preserve a sense of their self-worth and a positive image in the eyes of people they value. Placement in separate special provision has been argued to offer both a threat to, and an opportunity for children to maintain, their self-worth. On the one hand, segregation reduces the opportunities for unfavourable comparisons between the child who is segregated and other children who remain in the mainstream. On the other hand, segregation serves to accentuate the difference between segregated and non-segregated pupils, and confirms the devalued status of the former.

2.23   Children who are segregated have a number of options open to them to explain and manage their new status. One is to deny responsibility for it. David Galloway (1985) tells of a boy in a residential school for 'maladjusted' children who maintained that he could not help his bizarre behaviour because he was maladjusted. Thus he insisted that his status was beyond his control. Another strategy is to create a higher relative status by comparing yourself with others who have an even lower position in the hierarchy. Some of the children studied by Ince, Johnstone and Swann who were integrated into a comprehensive school maintained that not all their peers at the special school could be similarly integrated. One commented that 'most of them are in wheelchairs and haven't got the strength to pick up a pencil'. Another said, 'No, because some of them are mentally and physically handicapped'. A third strategy is to attempt to invert the status hierarchy altogether by asserting the value of characteristics possessed only by members of the segregated group. Adults with disabilities have found it important on occasions to revalue their identities in this way. Deaf people, for example, have increasingly asserted the value of their own language and culture. A fourth strategy is to find a new valued identity through an anti-school subculture. This strategy has been extensively observed in mainstream schools, but much less has been written about anti-school pupil subcultures in special schools and units.

2.24   The act of segregation is certainly not the sole cause of children's understandings about their segregated peers, or of segregated children's understandings of themselves, but it does have an impact. One of the arguments for integrating children from special into mainstream provision is that stereotypes would be harder to sustain. Faced with the evidence of individual children, interactions would develop on the basis of personal rather than group characteristics. We can see children beginning to respond to their peers on the basis of their individual rather than their group identity in some of the comments of children in Cassette Programme 2. But physical contact and geographical closeness alone will not eliminate negative stereotypes. Children who have been integrated into mainstream schools are sometimes subject to negative attitudes (see Gottlieb, 1975, for a review of studies of attitudes towards children with learning difficulties).

2.25   But there is evidence that personal contact can reduce negative stereotyping and lead to more individualized understandings of children with disabilities. Adrian Furnham and Maureen Gibbs (1984) found that 13- and 14-year-olds who had personal knowledge of someone with a disability were less likely to produce negative stereotypes. Will Swann (1987a) talked to a small group of children who were in the same class in a junior school as Samantha, a girl with multiple disabilities and learning difficulties. Samantha started her school career in the special care unit of a special school for children with severe learning difficulties. At the time of the study, she was a full-time member of her junior school, individually integrated. In response to the question 'What sort of person is Sam?', one of the children replied:

Well, she has her times, sometimes. When this new lady [Sam's new welfare assistant] came to look after her, she was crying 'cos she wanted her mum, 'cos it's like being with a stranger, and taken away from your mum and dad. So, really, she wasn't used to her. But she's getting used to her now. But she still has her times ... but she's OK. She's nice, you know. Once you get used to her you think, you know, more of her.

(Swann, 1987a, p. 306)

In fact it was quite difficult to evoke stereotyped descriptions of Samantha – a child who could not walk or communicate in spoken words, who had occasional epileptic fits and who was prone at the time to unprovoked screams. When another boy was asked how he would describe Sam to someone who didn't know her at all, he said 'Kind ... frightened ... nice.'

2.26 Our tendency to respond to people on the basis of stereotypes depends in part on the circumstances under which responses are required. Responses based on group identity are more likely to be evoked when group membership is significant. If integration continues to make group differences salient, then we might expect behaviour and attitudes towards the group to be more likely to depend on group characteristics. This is one reason why part-time integration schemes may not always reduce stereotyping. And if a group is integrated into a setting in which distinctions of ability are a dominant and pervasive way to respond to all children, then we might expect them to be subject to negative comparisons. If these children continue to be separately identified as a group, then we might also expect others to be more likely to respond to them on the basis of their group identity. If you would like to find out more about the operation of stereotypes in general and their impact on social identity, see Hewstone and Brown (1986) and Hogg and Abrams (1988).

The bottom of the pile

2.27 We have now considered some of the ways in which selection processes lead to distinctions in the school experience and social identities of different groups in mainstream and special provision. But what about life inside special provision? From the outside it is tempting to think that, once selected for special provision, further ranking and selection of pupils is superfluous. Yet it would be surprising if special schools were able to avoid the values which permeate the rest of the education system. The first reading for this unit describes the operation of selection into a special care unit in a special school for children with severe learning difficulties.

2.28 Special care units are occupied by children with difficulties and disabilities that are judged by staff to be particularly serious. In a survey of 43 special schools for children with severe learning difficulties, Peter Evans and Jean Ware found that 18 per cent of all the children in these schools were in special care units (SCUs):

most children ... are there, in the view of headteachers, because of a combination of lack of mobility, multiple handicaps, their absolute cognitive level and consequent high dependency and needs for high staff ratios. But about 50 per cent of them may be there for quite different reasons (chief amongst these is behaviour problems) and some, however well they 'qualify' according to other criteria, will not be placed in the SCU unless they fall within a certain age range.

(Evans and Ware, 1987, p. 45)

In 38 per cent of the schools surveyed by Evans and Ware, the special care unit was physically separate from the rest of the school, either as a distinct part of the main building, or in a separate building.

Activity 2   Layers of selection and segregation ──────────

Now read '"Totally impractical!": integrating "special care" within a special school' by Jenny Corbett (Reader 1, Chapter 17). In the second section, 'Just a matter of containing the children', Jenny Corbett gives an indication of the grossly inadequate provision for some children in special care in the early 1970s just after this group of pupils joined the education system. In 'Gaining control' she describes the way in which behaviourist methods were taken up at that time in this special care unit. Later on in this unit we shall be looking at these methods in more detail. As you read the next two sections, draw up a list of points of comparison between the processes of selection and stereotyping observed in this special school, and those we have already discussed.

──────────────────────────────

2.29   A number of aspects of life in this special care unit are mirrored by Evans and Ware's survey. They found that the majority of children in special care had multiple and profound disabilities, and were at a very early developmental level. But 'there are some children being educated in SCUs whom it is surprising to find there, given the generally held view of what a "special care" child is like' (Evans and Ware, 1987, p. 81). Summarizing other studies (Preddy and Mittler, 1981; Welsh Office, 1983), Evans and Ware concluded:

1   the proportion of children placed in special care varies widely from school to school;

2   not all profoundly retarded children are placed in the Special Care Unit;

3   there are often children more handicapped than some of those in special care in the main part of the school;

4   children placed in special care in one school would not necessarily be so placed in another school.

(Evans and Ware, 1987, p. 4)

2.30   The low status and morale of teachers in the special care unit Jenny Corbett describes was also a widespread problem identified by Evans and Ware:

> On the whole morale amongst the interviewed teachers was extremely low, although there were noticeable individual exceptions. They saw themselves as teaching a group of children who were regarded by even their SLD [severe learning difficulties] colleagues as 'different' at best, and ineducable at worst. They viewed their chances of promotion as being worse than those of their colleagues, and some of them ... also felt their chances of moving to another class, even within the same school, were poor.
>
> (Evans and Ware, 1987, p. 139)

2.31   There are similarities between the processes of selection we have already considered and those in this special school:

- placement in special care led to different treatment, including in this case the domination of life by routine care procedures, containment and control;

- the children in the unit became subject to a group identity ascribed to them by staff;

- selection led to reduced contact between the children in special care and other children;

- selection made the characteristics for which children were placed in special care, such as disruptiveness, more salient in the eyes of staff;

- judgements about individual children in special care were made on the basis of their group identity, rather than their personal identity – note that the child transferring from another school escaped the group identity;

- when some children were integrated into main school classes, staff reassessed their identities as individuals, but this did not remove the group identity of the special care unit.

Notice also how the processes of selection and stereotyping applied with equal force to the staff in the special care unit. In Unit 6/7 Section 2 we described the way in which learning support teachers in mainstream schools may be subject to similar processes.

THE IMPACT OF THE NATIONAL CURRICULUM

2.32   All the distinctions of experience that we have discussed so far need to be seen in the light of the principle that, in some way, all children should be treated similarly – that fundamental distinctions between children in the way they are educated are wrong. This belief was at the heart of the Warnock Report's proposals in 1978:

We hold that education has certain long-term goals, that it has a general point or purpose, which can be definitely, though generally, stated. The goals are twofold, different from each other, but by no means incompatible. They are, first, to enlarge a child's knowledge, experience and imaginative understanding, and thus his [sic] awareness of moral values and capacity for enjoyment; and secondly, to enable him to enter the world after formal education is over as an active participant in society and a responsible contributor to it, capable of achieving as much independence as possible. The educational needs of every child are determined in relation to these goals. We are fully aware that for some children the first of these goals can be approached only by minute, though for them highly significant steps, while the second may never be achieved. But this does not entail that for these children the goals are different. The purpose of education for all children is the same; the goals are the same.

(DES, 1978, p. 5)

2.33   Seven years after children with severe learning difficulties were first admitted to the education system, this statement was a powerful assertion of the common humanity of all children, even if the reality of life in schools rarely matched up to it then or now. The principle that at some level all children should receive the same curriculum has more recently received a powerful boost from the National Curriculum. The 1988 Education Reform Act set down for the first time in law a duty on all schools to provide a common curriculum for all children. Subsequently, the National Curriculum Council (NCC) declared that:

All pupils share the right to a broad and balanced curriculum, including the National Curriculum. The right extends to every registered pupil of compulsory school age attending a maintained or grant maintained school, whether or not he or she has a statement of special educational needs. This right is implicit in the 1988 Education Reform Act.

The range of needs to which this principle of entitlement applies will vary from the profound and multiple disabilities which are experienced by a minority of pupils and call for life-long support to the sometimes less apparent educational problems of those who, for example, have intermittent hearing loss.

(NCC, 1989, p. 1)

Does the National Curriculum ensure this principle of entitlement to a common curriculum? What impact will it have on the distinctions made in the education system between different groups of learners?

Activity 3   Entitlement and differentiation ————————————

Write down the arguments you can think of for seeing the National
Curriculum as a development that will reduce distinctions of experience
between groups of learners and the arguments that it will increase such
distinctions. If you can, compare your list with another student's.

———————————————————————————————————————

A common entitlement?

2.34   We have seen that special provision has been criticized for
sometimes providing children with a narrow curriculum. One of the
consequences of the National Curriculum is that it has helped to broaden
the curriculum in those schools which have offered a narrow diet in the
past, and it makes it rather more difficult for mainstream schools to
restrict the curriculum for children who experience learning difficulties.
One of the immediate effects in special schools for children described as
having moderate learning difficulties and emotional and behavioural
problems was a flood of interest in teaching science and technology.

2.35   It has also been suggested that the National Curriculum has helped
to raise expectations amongst teachers in special provision. For example,
Standard Assessment Tasks (SATs) for English at Key Stage 3 were
trialled in the summer of 1990 by one of the groups developing SATs.
When teachers in special schools were first presented with the material,
many said that their pupils would not be able to cope: it was too
difficult. There had been no separate material prepared for special
schools. In the event, most of the pupils enjoyed the material, found it
stimulating and challenging and responded much better than their
teachers had anticipated.

2.36   The National Curriculum has also begun to break down divisions
between special and mainstream provision in the way teachers think
about the curriculum. Special schools and units are not just physically
separate from mainstream schools, they are also organizationally
separate. They tend to have access to different LEA support staff.
Mainstream advisers and inspectors in some LEAs rarely visit special
schools, whose support in the LEA often comes mainly from educational
psychologists; they tend not to be part of mainstream information
networks, so that new curriculum projects often pass them by, through no
fault of the special school staff; inservice training for teachers (INSET)
from special schools is often provided separately from mainstream
INSET; there are separate professional organizations. All these factors
contribute to what we might call 'a curriculum culture' in special schools
that is rather different from the curriculum culture in ordinary schools.
The National Curriculum provided a sizeable injection of mainstream
curriculum thinking into special schools. Richard Byers describes some of
the changes faced by teachers in schools for pupils with severe learning
difficulties:

> This [the National Curriculum] must present teachers in schools for
> pupils with severe learning difficulties with a challenge.

Traditionally their approach has been founded upon the setting of tight, precise objectives, on the teaching of clearly defined individual skills, often one-to-one, with the rigorous assessment of progress informing the setting of further objectives. The work, in other words, is product-orientated – concerned with the new skills that children acquire and that can be observed and measured against various pre-arranged criteria. Indeed, special school teachers have, of late, sometimes taken to criticising themselves for being too prescriptive, too directive and too closed in their approach. It is possible that the very rigour which is applied to objectives-based teaching in schools for pupils with severe learning difficulties can cause skills to be taught out of context and children to become adult-dependent. Furthermore, choosing a variety of unrelated individual targets for each pupil from an array of subject-specific programmes does not always provide a coherent scheme of work for that child.

It is clear that the topic approach and the tradition of objectives-based teaching stand in contrast to one another and that both methodologies have their strengths and their disadvantages. The challenge facing teachers in special schools is to try to reconcile the two approaches, capitalising upon their advantages while avoiding the pitfalls of both.

(Byers, 1990, p. 110)

In Section 5 we shall look at the impact of the National Curriculum on this group of schools in more detail.

Increasing divisions?

2.37   The arguments so far support the view that the National Curriculum will encourage a common curricular entitlement. But there are also arguments that the National Curriculum will foster undesirable differentiation between children. These are discussed in the next reading.

Activity 4   On the level ───────────────────

Now read 'Hardening the hierarchies: the National Curriculum as a system of classification' by Will Swann (Reader 1, Chapter 7). In this chapter, Will Swann examines the way in which the National Curriculum has been organized into levels of attainment, and the origins and consequences of this structure. In the chapter's introduction there is a reference to 'disapplications and modifications' of the National Curriculum under Sections 17, 18 and 19 of the 1988 Education Reform Act. These are discussed later in the chapter in 'Legislating for learning progress'. You may find it useful to approach the chapter as offering one set of answers to the following questions:

(a) What motives led to the creation of the National Curriculum as we now have it?

(b) Why was the National Curriculum organized into ten levels of attainment?

(c) How did the subject working parties who created the detailed content of the curriculum for each subject deal with the task of dividing their part of the curriculum into ten levels?

(d) How and why did certain levels of attainment come to be linked to certain age groups?

(e) Does the National Curriculum support the development of a common curricular experience for all children?

You may well have thought about some or all of these questions before doing E242. If so, note down your own views before you read the chapter, and compare them with Will Swann's afterwards. Are you convinced by the arguments in the chapter, and if not, why not?

SUMMARY

(a) Grouping by attainment is a pervasive feature of mainstream schools which contributes to the creation of negative stereotypes of some pupils, and important distinctions between the school experience of different groups. In schools which have eliminated selective grouping, differences in attainment between pupils continue to be salient.

(b) Some special educational provision has been criticized for offering a limited curriculum and having low expectations of pupils.

(c) Children's presence in special provision can lead to a range of distinctions between their school experience and that of other pupils, which can serve to foster a separate group identity. In some cases pupils resent these distinctions.

(d) Separation of some children into special provision can contribute to the development of stereotypes held by teachers and pupils.

(e) Children who are placed in special provision may need to explain to themselves why they have been segregated, and actively manage any negative consequences.

(f) Whether integration reduces negative stereotyping may depend on the context into which children are integrated and the extent to which the group identity of the integrated pupils continues to be significant.

(g) Selection and grouping by attainment and other criteria can occur within special provision, with similar consequences to selection in mainstream schools.

(h) It has been argued that the National Curriculum will help to establish a common curricular entitlement for all children, thus reducing undesirable distinctions of experience. But it has also been argued that the organization of the National Curriculum into levels of attainment provides a resource for grouping children by attainment on partly arbitrary grounds, which will tend to increase distinctions of curricular experience.

3 ACCESS TO THE MAINSTREAM

3.1   In this section we are concerned with how children with disabilities can participate in diverse mainstream groups. You saw in Unit 1/2, in the study of the Grove school, that many factors are involved in enabling children with disabilities to participate fully in the life of a mainstream school. In this section we take up only a few of them that especially affect what happens in lessons. In Unit 16 we shall discuss the effects of the way schools are organized and staffed. Here we look first at the role of microtechnology. Then we discuss the many minor (and major) changes that may be needed to include children with visual disabilities in mainstream groups. Finally, we turn to issues raised by the participation of deaf children in mainstream lessons.

3.2   We can think of all the strategies we are going to discuss as giving children access to the curriculum. 'Access' is a very common metaphor, though it should be used with care. When we use the word 'access' outside education we think about being able to get to a place. Remote mountain villages are inaccessible; the main access to a country hotel is through a deer park, and so on. In carrying the word into educational jargon, we sometimes use it literally. Many schools are literally inaccessible for people who do not move about unaided on two legs. But more often we use the word metaphorically: 'gaining access to science' does not always mean getting into the science labs – it more often means 'doing science'. 'Access' suggests something or some place you are trying to get to by a specially made route. The discussion in Unit 6/7 raises some problems for this image. First of all, we saw examples of learning support teachers giving children access to a bad curriculum. Secondly, we saw several examples of the curriculum being shaped through negotiation between teachers and children. In these examples, children were not trying to get to some fixed set of classroom activities, they were helping to design them. (But we might also say that this does make knowledge accessible.) We chose to put the material in Unit 6/7 before the material in this unit to emphasize that responding to the diversity of learners is more than a matter of providing easy routes for individuals to an otherwise inaccessible curriculum. It may require more fundamental changes.

3.3   We saw in Unit 6/7 that many difficulties in learning arise because of communication breakdowns between teachers and pupils. Disabilities, and the way we respond to them, can be added sources of communication failure. A disability can have no effect on your capacity to communicate – or it can make it very difficult indeed. Many disabilities threaten children's ability to communicate, whether it is in the transitory form which most of us achieve through speech, or the more permanent form for which most of us rely on written text. Many responses to disabilities also put communication at risk. Adam Wright communicates through signing and a piece of microtechnology called a Lightwriter. He does not speak or understand the spoken word. He wrote this poem:

Faces of despair

People will talk,
to you as if you are,
of something different,

I enjoy talking,
but I can see the curious eyes,
that give you a stone gaze,
cold as winter, thin and flat,

Faces are fat and tired,
the eyes are like fishes swimming
in the stormy sea,

Boredom is followed by,
drifting into another world
of their own, as in a book.

They don't listen,
just pretending,
looking at you with
a hidden eye.

(Adam Wright, in Allen *et al.*, 1989, p. 69)

Through the means of communication he has been given Adam Wright indicts the failure of others to communicate with him. It is tempting to think that disability creates its own barriers to communication. Adam Wright's poem tells us that the ability to communicate is not a guarantee that others will wish to communicate with you, nor that you will gain entry to the places and events where, through communication, you become part of society. Attitudes and social practices can make an ordinary life terribly inaccessible.

Activity 5　Designing communication support

Below are three accounts of pupils whose disabilities give rise to communication problems. The accounts have been adapted from case studies written by staff of the CALL (Communication Aids for Language and Learning) Centre, in Edinburgh. The full accounts are in a microcomputer-based training and information resource produced by the Centre, and sold on disc (CALL, 1991). (The resource can also be used easily to produce printed materials.) All three pupils attended the CALL Centre for advice and support on their communication difficulties. As you read the accounts write down the factors that should be taken into account in designing communication support for these pupils. Group them into headings that seem appropriate to you.

Natalie

Natalie is 12. She attends a Scottish high school where she spends much of the day with the same small group of pupils, attached to the Learning Support Base, and integrates into the mainstream of the school for practical subjects such as science and home economics. She visited the CALL Centre in December 1988 to explore what form of technological support would be most appropriate as a writing aid. Natalie has mild cerebral palsy, which affects her balance and co-ordination and, in particular, the function of her right arm and hand. She uses her right hand for handwriting, but finds this very slow and laborious, and tires quickly. The longer she has to write, the slower and less legible her handwriting becomes. She has tried using typewriters and a scribe in school. She has used a conventional word-processor, but her learning support teacher felt she might need more help to write at higher speeds.

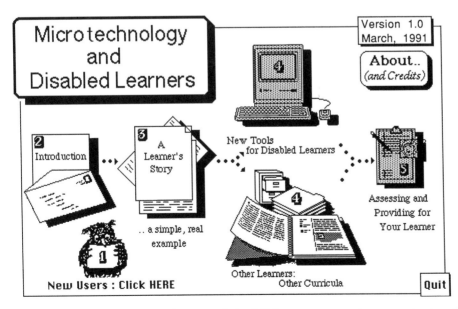

Figure 1　The 'contents page' screen of the CALL resource, a microcomputer-based training and information service (CALL, 1991).

Natalie is fairly familiar with the QWERTY keyboard and can type at about the same speed as she can handwrite. Her handwriting declines swiftly as her right hand tires, but with a keyboard she can continue with the left hand, occasionally using her right hand as well. Natalie's position at the keyboard is important. She needs a firm, highish chair and a built-up wedge-shaped wrist rest between her and the computer, to give stability and support to her wrists and the heel of her hands, allowing her to use gravity to drop her hands down on to the keys. This should reduce the fatigue.

At school Natalie needs to write mainly in order to copy short notes from the blackboard and to do written exercises in class and homework. She needs a writing aid which:

- she can carry by herself, in something like a shoulder-bag.

- can be operated by both hands.

- is powerful enough to allow storage of writing in memory, and basic editing facilities.

- can be connected to a printer.

- has a clear visual display. Although Natalie has no visual impairment, she has difficulties with reading and spelling, and so it is important that the screen should have the best possible contrast, definition of letters, and the fullest display of the writing she has already done, in the layout it will ultimately be printed in.

- is simple to use for all concerned: Natalie, her parents, and all her teachers, so they do not need extensive training.

After long and detailed assessment and discussion, staff at the CALL Centre, and from Natalie's school and LEA decided to try out a particular lightweight laptop computer with a built-in simple word-processor.

Gordon

Gordon is a 14-year-old at a special school. He has athetoid cerebral palsy. He has some difficulty in writing with a pencil or pen so he writes with a portable computer, which he uses in all of his classes. His speech is moderately impaired, though usually intelligible. Gordon's physics teacher had asked about help for Gordon as he is having difficulty laying out formulae and equations on his computer, which cannot generate the special symbols or Greek characters used in physics. Another problem is that when Gordon is working out the solution to a long expression, he can only see the last few steps in the process, because the screen is so small. Questions in exams often require the students to copy or fill in missing sections of diagrams. It would be useful if Gordon could do such exercises without relying on a scribe, because a stranger can sometimes have difficulty understanding him, and so he sometimes has to work out long calculations mentally before telling the scribe what to write. Gordon's teachers felt he should be able to do homework on the same system he uses at school. At present he leaves his computer in school so that the day's work can be printed out, and uses a typewriter at home.

Gordon's mathematics teacher highlighted similar problems. In one lesson the class were doing trigonometrical problems, and Gordon's method was to work out the result using a calculator and then type it out on the computer. The calculator buttons were very small, and it would be better if Gordon could use the computer to calculate the results, and the computer would then print it in the correct place on the screen.

In Gordon's chemistry class students need to take notes, write down chemical formulae, draw molecular structures, and draw diagrams of laboratory apparatus. The speed at which Gordon could produce work is important if he is to take notes during experiments.

Gordon's portable computer has a number of limitations which affect his performance. An ideal writing/drawing tool would be able to:

- generate mathematical and technical symbols, e.g. β, $\sqrt{(5y + 3z)}$.

- generate super and subscripts, e.g. $\tan^{-1}$, C_6.

- allow Gordon to lay out his equations neatly, using tabs, columns, and free movement of text and graphics.

- treat symbols as graphical objects to be moved around at will to produce diagrams.

- do scientific calculations and transfer the results directly to Gordon's current piece of work.

- provide some strategies for speeding up Gordon's writing. There are several methods of speeding up text production: for example, the storage of common words or phrases under code keys or abbreviations, or predictive systems.

- generate graphics, such as geometric shapes and laboratory equipment, and allow Gordon to manipulate and label them.

- produce a hard copy which matches the screen accurately, on normal A4 paper.

The device which provides all this must:

- be light and portable enough for Gordon to carry around from class to class, and from home to school.

- have a large enough screen to allow Gordon to see a reasonable amount of work at one time.

- be slick to operate so that all functions are available without having to swap discs or 'mess around'.

In early 1989, staff at the CALL Centre began to investigate the possibilities of various IBM compatible laptop computers and to search for the best combination of software packages for Gordon's needs before organizing a demonstration and trial at school.

Cathy

Cathy is 14, lively and sociable, but under-achieving and rather frustrated in her mainstream school. She has athetoid cerebral palsy, and no functional speech. In conversation, she uses a mixture of vocalizations, facial signals, manual signs (e.g., for numbers, she holds out the appropriate number of fingers), spelling and Bliss symbols. Bliss symbols are graphic images made of nine basic geometric shapes. Through size, orientation, position and combination these symbols convey different meanings. There is a basic vocabulary of about 2,500 words. Some Bliss symbols are shown in Figure 2. Cathy has a Bliss chart with symbols she points to. Her symbol use is largely restricted to single symbol indications followed by guesswork, questioning and interpretation by her listeners. Cathy also has a word board for pointing to, but this was primarily designed to teach her to read, and it duplicates the vocabulary of the Bliss chart.

Cathy spent a disproportionate amount of time searching for a way of saying what she obviously knew she wanted to say, and encouraging the guesswork of her listeners. Her communication was being impeded by a vocabulary on her Bliss board and word board which did not match her needs. Cathy needed a more personalized chart display, which mixed words, part and whole phrases, names and Bliss symbols, including cues for interaction strategies, such as 'That's nearly it but not quite; if you ask further questions you'll get there', or 'Sorry, but you've gone off on the wrong track – can we start that again?' Cathy will need some guidance on appropriate 'registers' of language – her burgeoning ability to spell out 'rude' words obviously motivates her, but permanent display of such words on a chart might cause problems. The answer may lie in part phrases where Cathy can spell a 'missing word' such as 'That's a load of ...' Another useful strategy is to include very general all-purpose phrases like 'I'm sorry, but I don't think so'; 'You might have to help me, please'; 'Come on!'; 'What do you mean?'; 'You can say that again!'

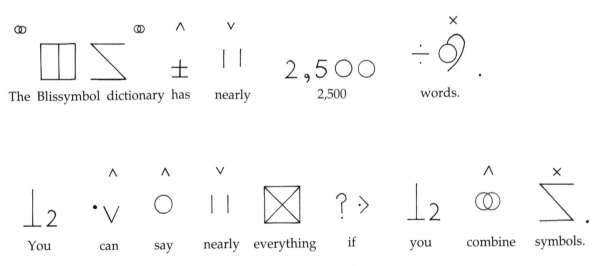

Figure 2   (courtesy Blissymbols Communication Resource Centre).

Cathy has got 'stuck' with sentence construction, working with formal and highly structured methods, so it seems reasonable to try to display a selection of fully formed phrases and sentences, to see if the use of sentences in communication is more motivating than trying to build them. This may be achieved to a certain extent on a personalized word chart but might also be developed through use of special software or an electronic communication aid.

Cathy may have become 'stuck' with reading and spelling because the materials used do not match her age level and her own communication goals. She summed it up herself once, by starting to spell out 'b–o–r–i–n– ... '. Language materials and tasks should be age-appropriate and meaningful to Cathy and this may mean stepping back from formal teaching exercises.

In 1987, staff at the CALL Centre recommended a more personalized and more portable (folding) communication chart for Cathy, among other computer-based tools aimed at helping her writing.

Assessing the need for communication support

The individual

3.4   Each of these three young people has disabilities which have to be understood in individual terms. The medical label attached to their disabilities on its own is not very revealing. Their requirements for communication support depend on their abilities, interests, personal goals and motivations, their social worlds and the social worlds they want access to, as much as on their disability. There is no point in providing access to something an individual doesn't want. Communication aids need to satisfy personal goals; they are not simply 'technical fixes' to overcome disability.

Learning demands

3.5   In school, children face demands for reading, writing, drawing, using special symbol systems like mathematical formulae, speaking, listening, and organizing time and work. Each learning task generates its own demands, and it is often only possible to understand exactly what these are by watching learners trying to cope with them. Sometimes this can give rise to questions about the suitability of the task for that learner even with communication support, if not for all learners in the class.

The context

3.6   We have to take account of the way communication support for a child will affect other people. Teachers need to be able to understand enough of the system the child is using to know how she uses it and what can be expected from her. Other children may also need to understand something of the system, so they can be conversational partners and collaborators in learning. The physical environment of the school also needs to be taken into account. The size and portability of a communication system is often very important.

Technology

3.7   Communication support is not necessarily complicated or electronic. It might be an extra pair of hands, like a classroom assistant to act as a scribe. It might involve improving and adapting furniture; minor changes to materials; a low tech aid, like a Bliss board. As we shall see below, for some learners with disabilities it might be a different language. Sometimes it does involve using clever technology. Being aware of the potential of technology is important: it can offer tools for writing, reading, drawing, speaking, listening, and controlling the environment. The next reading for this unit explores these possibilities, and says more about the issues we have already discussed.

Activity 6   The potential of microtechnology

Now read 'Expanding horizons: microtechnology and access to the National Curriculum' by Christopher and Rowena Onions (Reader 1, Chapter 14). In the section 'Access to the National Curriculum', the authors have organized the material around National Curriculum headings, and they expand on the ways in which microtechnology can be used for writing, speaking, science and mathematics. In the last two sections, 'Issues of equity' and 'Issues of participation and control', they discuss some of the wider questions raised by microtechnology which is available to some learners but not others. Before you read these two sections you might like to write down your reactions to these three statements:

- Microtechnology can give some learners with disabilities an unfair advantage.

- Children should be able to reject communication aids if they don't like them.

- Microtechnology can isolate people with disabilities from ordinary life.

MORE THAN TECHNOLOGY

3.8   The technologies we have described can make a great difference to children with disabilities. But technology alone does not create a supportive learning environment for any child with a disability. To see the range of other issues that may be involved, we shall consider what children who have visual disabilities may need in order to participate in mainstream lessons.

Microtechnology allows children to control a computer in many ways.

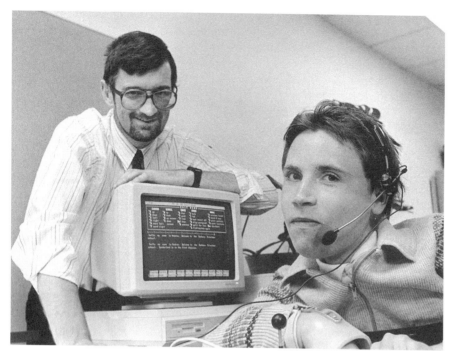

A voice-driven system

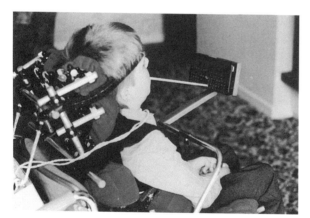

A mouthstick to input text.

Using a trackerball to draw.

Activity 7   How do you support a child with a visual disability?

Imagine you are a teacher in a primary or secondary school who is about to take on a child who has a visual disability. What changes might you expect to make in your classroom to include this child? Don't worry if you have no experience of children with visual disabilities. The purpose of this exercise is to get you to think actively about the issues. You may say that it depends on the child, in which case, write down exactly what you think it depends on.

3.9   Including a child who is blind or partially sighted may call for technological support, but it can also involve changes in the way a classroom is organized, the way learning materials are prepared, social relationships in the class, staffing, classroom equipment and how teachers talk to pupils.

The classroom environment

3.10   Classrooms are busy places with many obstacles to negotiate and resources to find. Children who can't find what they want by sight will have an easier time if resources and furniture are in the same place from day to day, if doors are not left ajar, and there are no objects hanging from the ceiling or on the floor that they have not been told about. If materials are labelled in large print or braille, or coded in some way that the child can see, then they may be easier to locate. Lighting in a room can be crucial. A room can be too bright as well as too dark. Some children cannot control the amount of light flowing into their eyes. Excessive glare, reflected from a shiny wall for example, can cause real problems. Window blinds may be important for such a pupil. Positioning within the room can also matter a lot: lines of vision and viewing distance must be taken into account; some children need the light behind them to minimize glare. The child's position in relation to the material they are using can also be important: if it is flat on a table, leaning over to see it closer can reduce the light on the object, and become uncomfortable. An adjustable reading stand to bring material up closer to vertical can help, as can a reading lamp. And sound matters as well: partially sighted children often have to depend on listening to understand what is going on, so background noise needs to be kept low. Looking and listening closely is tiring so engagement in lessons may fall off in the afternoon. And it can often take longer to complete tasks even when the child is fresh and alert.

Adapting teaching methods and materials

3.11   Materials may need to be modified, or children given some means to read them. Some children with visual disabilities use touch to collect information. There is a small number of children who use braille to read and write. Braille is an embossed code used to represent English. It is

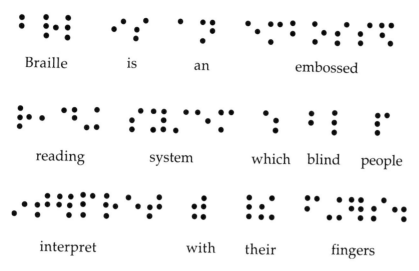

Braille   is   an   embossed

reading   system   which   blind   people

interpret   with   their   fingers

Figure 3   Grade II braille.

made up of sequences of six-dot patterns (see Figure 3). In Grade I braille, each character represents a letter, one of five common function words ('and', 'the', 'for', 'of', 'with') or punctuation. Grade II braille, for more skilled users, includes single braille letters that stand for words, abbreviations (for example, 'rcv' for receive) and contractions (a letter preceded by a special contraction sign) which indicate common parts of words, such as –tion. These devices speed up reading and writing. Before the advent of microcomputers, teachers who did not know braille had to arrange translations from a sighted braille user. Software is now available to make an automatic translation. The pupil uses a brailler that stores the information electronically. It can then be translated automatically, and printed out in conventional text. Equally, software can translate from stored text to Grade II braille printed out on a braille embosser.

3.12   Braille provides access to text, but not to graphic information. Tactile diagrams are one way of making graphic images accessible. These are made by producing a raised version of the diagram. Over this is laid a sheet of heat-sensitive plastic which is then moulded over the raised image in a 'thermoform' machine.

3.13   Increasingly, microtechnological solutions for children with disabilities are built around ordinary mainstream technology so that they enable children to use systems that schools already possess. For example, the Research Centre for the Education of the Visually Impaired at Birmingham University has produced software which is designed to provide speech-synthesized versions of text generated by mainstream word-processing, spreadsheet and database packages (Spencer and Ross, 1989). This software will produce a synthetic speech version of text, letter by letter or word by word. It will also read back any text which is brought onto the screen, making accessible teacher-produced materials prepared on a word-processor. In TV Programme 8, *Children First*, later in the course, you will see a pupil in a comprehensive school using such a system.

3.14   Some children with visual disabilities require less complex support. It is much easier for many partially sighted children to read teacher-produced material like worksheets if there is a strong contrast between the paper and the text. Inking over the text can make a great deal of difference. It is easier for some children who are partially sighted to see text, pictures and diagrams if they are enlarged. Many conventional photocopiers will do this job. Some material may need to be put on tape, and pupils may need to take notes with a cassette recorder. Mark is a six-year-old with very limited vision at a first school. This is what his class teacher provided for one morning's maths:

> The table was laid out with the group's wordcards and materials: a box of coloured counters, a box of the numbers 1 to 10 written on small squares of card, pencils and crayons, and the set-space mats [simple mathematical equipment]. At Mark's place was a workbook that Andrea [his teacher] had specially prepared. Mark had earlier done this activity using standard squared paper and had found it difficult to write in the small squares. Today the paper was marked in larger squares. The date was already written in large black letters at the top of the page. This had not been done for any other child. Six prominent pink dots were marked to indicate where Mark should record his sums, and Mark's pencil, sheathed in a rubber grip, had been placed on his book, another detail not provided for the others.
>
> (Swann, 1987b, p. 223)

3.15   Classroom language may also need to adapt. Often instructions and explanations from a teacher only make sense when you can see what they refer to, so instructions for a child with a visual impairment may need to be more explicit. As we saw in Unit 6/7, this can help all pupils. Children often pick up clues about what they are supposed to be doing by watching their peers; this is harder for partially sighted children. Like any other child, they may be reluctant to say they don't understand, and risk exposure. So they may need special attention to make sure they have understood what they have to do.

Working with other pupils

3.16   The success of any child at school depends to some extent on the attitudes and actions of other pupils. Children in the classroom may need simple accurate explanations of the difficulties that a disability creates. Teachers can help to promote appropriate unpatronizing interaction and avoid the danger of a child with a visual impairment becoming dependent on other children. When pupils are working together it is important to know who is in the group, who comes and who goes, otherwise joining the conversation can be difficult. With unfamiliar voices, a name at the beginning of each contribution helps to locate members of the group. Sometimes tasks can be structured so that a child with a visual disability plays an essential role in the group. Darren, a blind boy in an upper junior group at Castlecroft Primary School, Wolverhampton, used a microcomputer workstation linked to a brailler:

> The workstation proved to be an excellent 'group noticeboard', with the monitor screen clear for all to see.
>
> For example, Darren and a group of some sixteen other children were involved in a poetry writing session. The teacher presented the task, to record reactions to a visit to the river. The children were divided into groups and asked to collect words and images which would be appropriate. These were to be collected by one member of the group and would later report back to the whole teaching group. Because of the size of the workstation a group was formed around Darren, who was then able to record the ideas of the whole group via his Perkins Brailler and onto the monitor.
>
> (Watson and Vincent, 1987, p. 98)

Support staff

3.17   For many children with a visual disability, a classroom assistant is an important resource. Sarah is a seven-year-old who attends a first school supported by a classroom assistant for part of the day. Her classroom assistant does many jobs, listed below. Sarah is also visited regularly by a support teacher for the visually impaired who works in many schools in the area. She provides advice on teaching strategies, equipment and materials.

Helping Sarah to organize her work

The classroom assistant makes sure Sarah understands what she has to do and ensures that she has the necessary resources to hand. She helps Sarah to plan her work and maintain her concentration, and she reads material that Sarah cannot read herself.

Encouraging participation

Sarah is very quiet and tends not to take part in discussion. Her classroom assistant encourages her to join in and encourages other children to involve her in shared tasks. She also encourages Sarah to say when she does not understand what her teacher wants her to do.

Individual support

Sarah spends a short time every day individually with her classroom assistant on reading and writing tasks. In the near future she will learn to use a keyboard, which will become more important for her when she reaches secondary school. Her classroom assistant will teach her keyboard skills. She also spends some time adapting classroom materials, inking over some texts in black to improve contrast and enlarging others with the photocopier.

3.18   The proportion of children with hearing difficulties in mainstream schools rose substantially in the 1970s and 1980s as teachers of the deaf in many LEAs began to argue for the benefits of mainstream education for deaf children's language development. The majority of children described as partially hearing are now in mainstream schools, either in partially hearing units, or individually integrated. Fewer pupils categorized as deaf are in mainstream schools: at the end of the 1980s the majority were still in special schools, although numbers in special schools had declined steadily up to that point.

3.19   Deafness is a continuum, from those who hear no speech sounds, to those who lose only a small amount of significant auditory information. An audiogram is a standard way to indicate some of the important features of a person's hearing disability. An example is shown in Figure 4. Hearing loss is plotted as a graph with frequency of sound marked on the horizontal axis in hertz (Hz) and the amount of hearing loss along the vertical axis in decibels (dB). When a child has a greater than 30 dB loss she may have hearing difficulties in the classroom. As a guide, one can think of a loss of 30–70 dB as moderate, 80–100 as severe and above 100 as profound deafness. Hearing losses are rarely even across the whole speech frequency range. Much more information about speech is carried in the higher frequencies. For example, the telephone cuts out all frequencies lower than 330 Hz and that has no effect on the comprehensibility of speech. By contrast speech with frequencies over 2,000 Hz cut out by electronic means is very difficult to understand. Consequently, high frequency loss is of far greater significance than a loss in the lower frequency range.

Natural auralism

3.20   To many teachers of the deaf, integration into mainstream schools offers deaf children an environment which will foster their communication through spoken English, and give them access to the hearing world when they leave school. In the 1980s, Leicestershire was one LEA that pursued a policy of integration on these lines, as the head of service for hearing-impaired children explains:

> Leicestershire provides two main forms of special educational provision for hearing-impaired children – units catering for small groups of children attached to selected primary and secondary schools and local school placement supported by specialist visiting teachers. The integration of hearing-impaired children into the normal educational system is seen as a fundamental aspect of the development of the child as a member of the family, the community in which the family lives and the broad society of the United Kingdom. Fundamental to the satisfactory achievement of that integration however, is the acquisition of fluency in spoken language – the tool of communication of that society – yet that

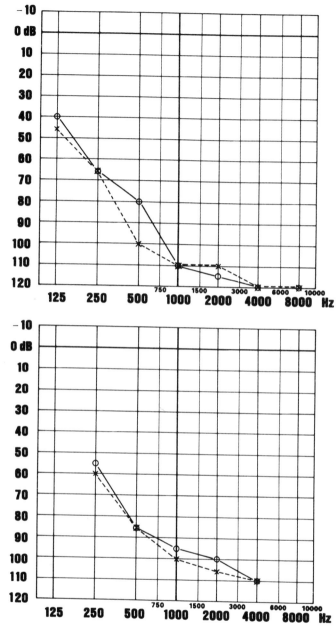

KEY: —o— Right ear

---x--- Left ear

Figure 4 Pure tone audiograms for two children who are profoundly deaf.

fluency in spoken language is itself a product of interaction in an auditory and verbal environment.

Integration is therefore seen as an integral part of a natural auditory approach to the development of spoken language in hearing-impaired children, as well as a means of exposing the child to normal levels of academic and social achievement.

(Harrison, 1986, p. 96)

3.21   The 'natural auditory' approach, often called 'natural auralism', has increasingly replaced a strategy which sought to teach deaf children to speak through structured language lessons in which children were given practice in specific features of English articulation, vocabulary and grammar. Natural auralism depends on two principles. The first is that children should make maximum use of their residual hearing through appropriate, well fitted and frequently checked hearing aids. The second is described by Conrad Powell, of the National Aural Group, which is devoted to the promotion of natural auralism:

> the provision of a rich linguistic environment offering natural language patterns at a normal rate of utterance and with normal intonation, rhythm and stress patterns …

> What must take place is real communication, spontaneous and motivated. The adults in a child's environment must create a situation in which language is acquired through meaningful linguistic input in play and other activities appropriate to the child's age. In other words, natural auralism has nothing to do with teaching language, but everything to do with providing a stimulating environment so that children are motivated to acquire language. Any subject in the school curriculum is a vehicle for language and thus knowledge, skills and language are all developed simultaneously.
>
> (Powell, 1989, p. 11)

3.22   In assessing the consequences of such broad principles, we need to look at classroom practice. Susan Gregory and Juliet Bishop (1988) studied the classroom experience of children with severe and profound hearing losses in primary schools where natural auralism was advocated. In the lessons they observed, teachers and deaf pupils had marked difficulty understanding each other. The following dialogue is an example:

> The teacher is talking about when the children were newborn babies in hospital. According to the conventions of maternity hospitals they would have been known as 'baby + surname'. The teacher goes around the class saying to each one 'What would you have been called? Baby … ?' Each replies Baby and then their own surname. None of them had any problem with this except Katherine, who after many attempts by the teacher, is still unable to answer and has finally to be told.

> TEACHER: What would you have been called?
>
> KATHERINE: I don't know
>
> TEACHER: What's your name?
>
> KATHERINE: ??? (indecipherable utterance)
>
> TEACHER: Baby Ash … ?
>
> KATHERINE: Ash
>
> TEACHER: What's your second name? What comes after Katherine?
>
> KATHERINE: (no response)

TEACHER: Baby who?

KATHERINE: Ash

TEACHER: Ash de. Come on.

KATHERINE: Ash de.

TEACHER: Ash de, I'll give you Ash de. Ash who? What's your second name? Katherine Ash de?

ANOTHER CHILD: Down.

KATHERINE: Ash de.

TEACHER: Ashdown isn't it? So you would have been 'Baby Ashdown'.

KATHERINE: (laughs)

(Gregory and Bishop, 1988)

3.23   In the classrooms studied by Gregory and Bishop the deaf children used a variety of strategies to 'get by', which, whilst often effective in the short term, had the effect of hiding their difficulties. These included nodding or shaking the head in response to questions; repeating the last thing said; giving the name of a colour relevant in the context; using contextual clues such as pictures to guess what was required. Gregory and Bishop describe teachers and children 'colluding with each other in maintaining the semblance of classroom interaction, when for neither party is the communication based in mutual understanding'. The communication difficulties which they identified were profound, pervasive and occurred for many children in many classrooms. You may find it useful to compare the interaction between Katherine and her teacher with the examples of classroom interaction used in Unit 6/7, Section 5, which show the asymmetry of power in teacher–pupil dialogue. David Wood and his colleagues (1986) have shown how changes in teachers' conversational style with deaf children which reduced the teacher's control of the dialogue led to much greater participation by deaf children, who produced longer, more animated and interesting contributions. So the dialogues and difficulties revealed by Gregory and Bishop should not be taken as inevitable consequences of deaf children's participation in mainstream lessons under natural auralism.

Bilingualism

3.24   But the classroom consequences of natural auralism are only part of a much larger picture. Debates about the education of deaf children are intimately connected to debates about the place of deaf people in society. In saying that deaf children should become members of 'the community in which the family lives and the broad society of the United Kingdom', Harrison prescribes social and cultural aspirations for those children. He omits aspirations to join social worlds that many deaf people see as vital to their lives. The deaf community in this country, as in many others, is a distinct cultural grouping, with its own history, traditions, values, ways of living and language. The language of the deaf community in the UK is British Sign Language (BSL; see Figure 5). BSL is a distinct language as

Name   Cheat   Far

Bird   Praise   Good

Bad   Criticize

Figure 5   Some BSL words. Drawings cannot convey the complex grammatical structure of the language.

different from English as are French and Urdu; indeed, in many respects it is more distinct for it uses the visual-spatial medium to convey meaning as well as the temporal sequence and structure of components on which spoken languages rely. BSL is not English in signed form, and the two cannot be used simultaneously.

3.25   Deaf culture and BSL have been the subject of prejudice and suppression, especially from teachers of the deaf, for much of the twentieth century. Only fairly recently have linguists studied and revealed to BSL and non-BSL users alike the complexities and sophistication of the language (Brennan, 1987; Kyle and Woll, 1985). For a long time, BSL was thought by many teachers of the deaf to be a substandard form of language, incapable of communicating complex meaning (see Lane, 1984). In 1985, Tony Booth collected these examples of prejudice towards deaf people amongst teachers of the deaf in part of Scotland:

> One teacher of the deaf referred to the adult deaf community as the 'deaffies' and to one deaf man who had the temerity to challenge her as 'some deaf Jamie'. Another spoke of the use of sign language as akin to 'barking at print for hearing children'; having the surface trappings of a real skill but without the involvement of comprehension ... Another suggested that signing challenged God's physiological acumen: 'If he had meant us to sign, the functions of language would not have been organized in the left hemisphere of the brain'. Another educator, an ex-headteacher of a school for the deaf, went even further. He moved from a discussion of the medieval doubt of the presence of a soul in the deaf to a sudden espousal of his own present views:
>
>> If you look at a Minister signing the Lord's Prayer it can look beautifully expressive – but what does that waggling of hands mean to the deaf? No-one knows what they are thinking about. We were not intended to learn the language of signs ... Faith can only come through hearing ... isn't it a fact that faith was transmitted orally?
>
> (Booth, 1988, p. 109)

3.26   Some deaf people are vehemently opposed to the integration of deaf pupils. They argue that integration involves the break-up of communities of deaf children who share a common language in BSL. Special schools form part of the communication network of the deaf community. For a long time they were almost exclusively oralist, although signing flourished surreptitiously in the pupils' own subculture. More recently special schools have become increasingly open towards signing and BSL. Many have adopted 'total communication' methods. What this means in practice varies from school to school. It may involve the use of whatever means are available to communicate: this includes speech, lip-reading and various forms of signing. However, the objective is principally communication in English, whether spoken or signed. The deaf community and its supporters have increasingly argued for a bilingual approach to their education with BSL as the first language and principle medium of instruction for deaf children, and English as a second language. They argue that this is a better way to enable deaf children to learn. BSL is inherently better suited to them than English, and so they can acquire a language through which they can learn, rather than be hampered by failing to grasp any language sufficiently to cope with the demands of the classroom. Bilingualism also gives deaf children access to the deaf community.

3.27   One area which has introduced a policy which combines bilingualism with integration is Leeds, where total communication has been redefined to include BSL as a distinct medium of instruction. According to Miranda Pickersgill, the head of the Leeds service for the hearing-impaired: 'We acknowledge that it is very hard for deaf children to learn English or another spoken tongue ... They will do better if they are first given sign language within a bilingual context' (quoted in O'Grady, 1990, p. 11). In the late 1980s Leeds established nine schools, primary, middle and secondary, as 'resource schools', each of which has a resource base for deaf pupils. Children integrate into mainstream classes, and do some withdrawal work in the resource base. Each resource school has one or more support teachers of the deaf, and there are deaf instructors and BSL/English interpreters shared between schools. In the next activity, you will read a short description of how this policy has been put into practice in one primary school.

Activity 8   Signing in the mainstream

Now read 'Signing and talking in a Leeds primary school' by Beate Schmidt-Rohlfing (Reader 1, Chapter 13). This chapter describes some of the school experiences of one deaf girl whose language environment involves three languages. As you read, note the communication problems that Asima experiences, and the role of BSL in tackling these problems. Note too the strategies that Schmidt-Rohlfing suggests to overcome some of the difficulties Asima still encounters. You may find it useful to relate the issues raised in this chapter to those raised by John Williamson in his discussion of support for bilingual pupils (Reader 1, Chapter 10, which you read in Unit 6/7).

SUMMARY

(a) Disability and people's response to disability pose threats to communication. Overcoming these threats to communication in schools can involve changing attitudes to disability as well as providing a range of individual supports to children with disabilities.

(b) Microtechnology offers powerful means to make it easier for some people with disabilities to speak, listen, read, write, draw and control their environment. In designing communication supports, it is important to take into account the learner's personal goals, the learning tasks she will face, and the context in which she will be learning, as well as her disability and its consequences. Solutions do not necessarily involve complex technology.

(c) Including a child with a disability in the mainstream curriculum may involve much more than individual communication supports. In the case of children with visual disabilities, it may call for changes in the classroom environment, modifications to teaching material and classroom talk, attention to relationships between pupils, and it may involve extra staff to support the teacher and pupil.

(d) How children who are deaf should be given access to the curriculum is a contentious issue. Much of the debate centres on whether the medium of instruction should be English or BSL, and if English, how its signed and spoken forms should be combined. But however this question is resolved, there remain many issues about the most appropriate teaching methods and forms of support.

4 PREPARING FOR THE MAINSTREAM: CONDUCTIVE EDUCATION

4.1   Many of the special arrangements we discussed in Section 3 are designed to allow children with disabilities to participate in the mainstream curriculum for most or all of the time, throughout their school career. They provide access to the mainstream from the start. But we can think of access in another way. It has been argued that some children need to spend some time preparing for the mainstream curriculum, because they lack the skills and attainments to take part in it. The job of special provision is to provide these children with the skills they will need when they enter the mainstream at some point in the future. This argument has been used to defend many different forms of separate special education, including full-time remedial education. It is said that to move some children straight into the mainstream curriculum would be counterproductive because they would not be able to make use of the learning opportunities it offers and would not acquire the means to do so. In some cases this argument is used to justify full-time segregation into a special school. In Section 3 of Unit 6/7 we discussed the arguments that led schools and LEAs to question remedial education as a preparation for the mainstream curriculum. You may find it useful to remind yourself of these arguments, listed in the summary to that section.

4.2   The standpoint we adopt on such arguments depends in part on how flexible we think that the mainstream curriculum should be, which groups of children we are concerned with, and what kinds of preparation for the mainstream we have in mind. Arguments which tell against remedial education might not apply with equal force to other kinds of preparation for the mainstream. For example, what about a deaf child undergoing an intensive period of learning BSL in the early primary years as a preparation for bilingual mainstream education later on? Could such a period of separate education be justified on the grounds that it allows much greater participation in the mainstream and for a longer period than would be possible without it?

4.3   Some teachers in special schools who have made significant progress in integrating children with disabilities into mainstream schools argue just this kind of case. Tim Southgate is the head of Ormerod Special School in Oxford. This school supports large numbers of its pupils in full-time placements in mainstream schools. Its secondary department is based in a comprehensive school. In Unit 16 you will read Tim Southgate's account of the development of this school's policies. But he also argues that in the nursery and early primary years there is a case for full-time special school attendance for some children with physical disabilities to give them intensive early intervention which will later help them to be successful participants in the mainstream schools. During this time his school uses an approach known as conductive education. In this section we discuss this approach as an example of a special curriculum which aims to prepare children for the mainstream. Later in the section we look briefly at the arguments and evidence that we might demand of any proponent of a special curriculum which is designed to prepare children for the mainstream.

WHAT IS CONDUCTIVE EDUCATION?

4.4   The aim of conductive education is to teach children (and adults) with physical disabilities to move and control their bodies independently, without the help of aids and specialized equipment. It is an intensive, full-time programme. At the start of the 1980s it was known to only a small number of physiotherapists and teachers working with children with physical disabilities; ten years later it was much more widely known in professional circles, and amongst parents of children with disabilities. The intense interest in the method is based on the remarkable results that have been achieved in Hungary, where it originates. There are children in the UK whose disabilities are seen by professionals as preventing them from ever learning to move about independently. It is reported that in Hungary children with similar disabilities have learnt to do so. On the basis of this evidence, some parents have taken their children to Budapest to benefit from conductive education.

Activity 9   What is conductive education?

Now read the introduction to 'Conductive education: contrasting perspectives' (Reader 1, Chapter 16, pp. 183–7). This explains the background to the method, the principles on which it is based, and describes its main features.

4.5   In 1990 the first British school to use conductive education with the intensity and rigour of Hungarian practice, based in Birmingham, had eighteen children on roll, all aged between four and seven and all living locally. Being a day school the routine is slightly different from the Institute in Budapest. Mike Lambert, headteacher at the school, describes what happens:

> The routine starts early with the arrival of the first conductor at 8.00, to make the rooms ready for the group's activity. By 8.30 the first children are arriving, brought by taxi from their homes in Birmingham and nearby parts of the West Midlands.
>
> Having made their way to their places in the group room, the children change into simple T-shirts and shorts, clothing which facilitates independent action in movement and self-care and which is easily changed if toileting 'accidents' occur (no incontinence nappies are used at the Institute). The children use the potties or the toilet, the first of regular times throughout the day, then sit by the slatted tables or 'plinths' and talk and play.
>
> By 9.15 all have arrived, books and toys are collected up to make ready for calling the register. Then children stand to answer their names, help to change the day and weather charts, and give interesting items of 'news' for all to hear.
>
> By 9.30 the plinth programme is under way, a series of movement learning tasks, based round the plinths – stretching, bending, turning, rolling, pushing off to standing, down to sitting. 10.30 is refreshment time – a drink and toast or fruit. The children then hear plans for the walking programme. Sub-groups of three or four children work on tasks which lead to the attainment of independent walking.
>
> (Lambert, 1989, p. 14)

4.6   Conductive education makes considerable demands upon both conductors and pupils, but the staff at Birmingham clearly find the work very rewarding. A new teacher to the school stated, 'Conductive education has restored my faith in what teaching should be' (Taylor, 1989, p. 15). Lambert describes the conductor's tasks at the Birmingham school:

> Each conductor takes responsibility for a part of the day's programme. She must clarify its learning tasks, prepare its activity, the materials to be used, also, very importantly, the songs, stories, rhymes or games which are an invitation to the children to participate and do well in the tasks ahead. The ideal is a seamless routine where the emphasis of learning may change but where the features of the group activity and conductor behaviour remain constant, and where movement, speech, social and academic learning occur and are reinforced throughout the day.
>
> (Lambert, 1989, p. 15)

Conductive education in action at the Birmingham Institute.

4.7   As Mike Lambert (1990) describes, transferring conductive education from Hungary to Birmingham was not easy. Staff had to adjust to cultural differences during their training. In 1988, fourteen British trainees started a four-year course, working in both Hungary and Birmingham. They had to adjust to new, more demanding expectations of the children. Conductors in Hungary tended to see the needs of the whole group, not the individual, something that was difficult for British teachers to accept. Whereas the British trainees were all trained teachers from special or mainstream schools, Hungarian trainees were eighteen-year-olds, straight from school. Trainees were expected to observe and assimilate, not to be told what to do: conductive education was something done rather than talked about. British trainees had to unlearn some skills and start back at the beginning. It seems unsurprising, considering these difficulties, the demands of long shifts and the learning in a new language, that five of the fourteen dropped out.

4.8   Lambert also identifies professional barriers within the UK to introducing conductive education. It has not met with wholehearted approval in all circles. He found that some children at the Birmingham Institute were influenced by negative attitudes from professionals, as, for example, when their doctor would not support the programme. The role of a conductor also poses a threat to existing professional boundaries in the UK, where 'therapy' and 'teaching' are provided by two distinct professions. To train a new profession which claims to be able to do both of these, and suggests that it might be able to do the job better, is to challenge existing practice. But Lambert suggested that hostility towards conductive education in Britain had lessened and it was already, in 1990, being adopted by several institutions.

OPPRESSION OR LIBERATION?

4.9   According to Mike Lambert, the aims of conductive education are:

> to educate the minds of motor-disordered children so they can achieve the customary milestones of childhood and thus prepare for normal education and normal life. Not to manoeuvre a wheelchair but to walk, not to use artificial means of communication but to talk, not to manage incontinence but to be continent, not to retreat from intellectual demands but to look towards normal requirements and seek to attain them as do their able-bodied peers.
>
> (Lambert, 1989, p. 15)

'Normal life', for Lambert, does not include wheelchairs, alternative means of communication and incontinence. We can think of two different senses of the word 'normal'. The first is descriptive and statistical: what is normal is what most people are like and what they do. The second is prescriptive: what is normal is what people should do and should be like; abnormality, in this sense, is undesirable. These two senses of normality do not go together. Some activities which are statistically commonplace, like adolescent petty crime, are not desirable. Many activities, practised by only a very few people, such as breeding fancy rats or orchid growing, would not generally be described as 'abnormal' because they are not considered undesirable. When Mike Lambert defines the goals of conductive education he is not just commenting on the scarcity of wheelchairs. He implies that it is more desirable for children with physical disabilities to be able to walk than to use a wheelchair, more desirable for them to talk than to use alternative means of communication, more desirable for them to be continent than not. These are contentious opinions. For some writers, like the author of the next reading, these views, and the teaching methods derived from them, are oppressive.

Activity 10   Conductive education as oppression

Now read the second part of 'Conductive education: contrasting perspectives' by Mike Oliver: 'Conductive education: if it wasn't so sad it would be funny' (Reader 1, Chapter 16, pp. 187–90). Oliver writes as a person with a disability: he has a spinal injury that prevents him from walking. As you read, write down the key elements of his argument. If you have not read work on the politics of disability, you may find Mike Oliver's writing surprising, even shocking. If you do, try to explore why you are surprised or shocked. Which of your own views on disability are challenged?

4.10   Mike Oliver describes conductive education as 'theoretically unproven, practically unsubstantiated, and ideologically unsound'.

'Theoretically unproven'

4.11   Oliver's first argument is that the underlying theory of how the nervous system works is false. Mária Hári claims that the central nervous system can 'restructure itself'. Oliver says it cannot. What does 'restructure itself' mean? What evidence would you want to see to decide who is right? If 'restructure itself' means that a person whose brain has been injured can learn to do things in ways that circumvent the effects of the injury to the brain, then this is certainly true in some cases. And as Oliver points out, problems with the theory are not fatal to the teaching method. After all, the way most learning happens is poorly understood. Difficulty in explaining how teaching works is not an argument for refusing to teach.

'Practically unsubstantiated'

4.12   Oliver's argument here is not that conductive education fails to achieve results. He accepts that it does. It is that these results might be produced by other methods that have the same level of resourcing, which encourage active learning, and have a purposeful environment. Does this count against conductive education? Could an advocate reply: 'What does it matter, if it works?'

'Ideologically unsound'

4.13   This is the most important element in Oliver's case. The fact that conductive education helps some children with disabilities to move independently is not at issue. But should we regard this as a success? Oliver does not. He argues that in accepting a restricted definition of 'normality' as a goal in teaching children with disabilities, we force them to conform to standards which do not suit them, which are difficult to achieve and unnecessary. In forcing this definition of normality on people with disabilities we reinforce it as the standard to which all should aspire. But since some people cannot achieve this goal, or will do so only with great difficulty, the effect is to mark their failure to conform to the norm. Instead of seeking to force everyone to fit the same limited ideal of able-bodied normality, we should change our definition of normality so that it includes physical disability: we should learn to accept, even value, such differences. In this view, conductive education is based on prejudice which is akin to racism: it implies that it is unacceptable in able-bodied society to have a disability, just as it is unacceptable in some sectors of white society to be black.

4.14   Another argument Oliver makes is that conductive education demands individual changes in children, but does not tackle social changes that would benefit people with disabilities, such as making buildings more accessible. Do you think this is a valid criticism of conductive education? Could a method like conductive education make it more difficult to introduce social changes that would benefit people with disabilities?

4.15   Not all adults with disabilities share Mike Oliver's views. Some seek conductive education to try to overcome their disabilities. In the following dialogue from the BBC2 programme *One in Four*, broadcast in 1989, Chris Davies spoke to Angela Smith. Both have cerebral palsy but have very different views about their condition.

> CHRIS: Angela Smith, an Essex University student, is in Budapest now, spending a year, largely at her own expense, experiencing conductive education. She's been out there a couple of times before to be assessed and to sample the treatment, before making this longer commitment. Especially as we share the same disability I was curious to find out why Angela was so keen to go back for a full course.
>
> ANGELA: Conductive education is nothing like the physio I had as a child. I mean, what I had as a child was good, my specialist was very good, she did make sure I got the best of what was available at the time, but it clearly wasn't conductive education. The main difference is the physio that I got was relatively passive in the way that it was mainly having things done to me, whereas conductive education, they make you do things, they instruct you how to do things yourself.

CHRIS: While you were there were you given any impression that this was going to be in any way a miracle cure?

ANGELA: No, never. Those words shouldn't be ever used in relation to conductive education. It isn't, doesn't cure; even if a child or an adult seems to have got over their difficulty, they haven't been cured. They have just been taught to master their disability. For instance, before I went, my arms were a lot less controlled than after my first visit. I couldn't pick anything up without my arms flying all over the place. My typing speed's improved, which makes writing essays a lot easier now. My speech was easier to understand and I found it easier to speak. And also I must stress I could walk before I went out, but my balance was very poor, and that improved immensely. And also my standing posture was much straighter.

CHRIS: I have, I must confess, a small problem in understanding why you need to go because we both share the same disability and the same degree of disability largely, and yet although in an ideal world I wouldn't want to have my disability, I was brought up to think that it was unreasonable to expect something which was beyond me, and so I should be satisfied and make the most of what I have got. If I was born again, I perhaps wouldn't want to be like this, but I am, so I don't want anything more than I can actually have. So why do you want to be more than you actually are? Is it because you don't actually like being disabled? Do you resent being disabled?

ANGELA: Now you are getting to the root of it. I mean, I am only speaking personally. I suppose the basic reason I have taken it on is because deep down I don't. I have never really accepted my disability. I don't like being disabled. So any chance or opportunity I have to minimize it, I take it, as long as the cost isn't too high.

CHRIS: Don't you like being disabled? You and I have never experienced anything but the disability we have got, so what yardstick have you got for making you want to be something you have never experienced?

ANGELA: Because I can see that there is another way. I mean, the way I am, I am always coming up against frustrations, frustrations that I know that if I didn't have my disability I would not have to go through. OK, I know to be able-bodied isn't to have no problems, but I also know that they don't have to endure the kind of frustrations that someone like me and you have to. Whatever happens, I won't come back minus my cerebral palsy, but I am more confident that I will come back with a lot more control. It will enable me to get through life with less frustration and difficulty than I have to endure now.

CHRIS: Let's take the bull by the horns. People who are watching this interview might say 'Well, of course it must be terrible being disabled. We can't blame her for wanting to be less so', and other people might be very full of pity and sympathy towards you. How would you react to that kind of attitude?

ANGELA: Well, they can get rid of their pity and sympathy – I don't need it. I mean it is not so unbearable that I am constantly thinking of slashing my wrists. I am saying it is frustrating and although I get by and I have got myself to university, I am just saying that personally I find it hard to handle, and although I support disabled people who are coming out and saying they are not the same and should be accepted the way they are, I am still saying that if a chance comes along for me personally to overcome my disability, I will try it.

(BBC2, *One in Four*, 1989)

4.16   How do you react to Angela's combined support for disabled people's demands to be accepted the way they are, and her wish to overcome her disability? Does conductive education discourage able-bodied people from accepting people with disabilities as part of ordinary life?

Activity 11   Conductive education as liberation ————————

Now read the third part of 'Conductive education: contrasting perspectives' by Virginia Beardshaw: 'Conductive education: a rejoinder' (Reader 1, Chapter 16, pp. 190–92). Virginia Beardshaw has a daughter with a disability whom she has taken to Budapest. Make a note of the points on which she agrees and disagrees with Mike Oliver.

——

4.17   Virginia Beardshaw and Mike Oliver both object to the way that our society's limited definition of normality excludes people with disabilities and they are both very strong critics of current British rehabilitation methods. But whereas Mike Oliver argues that conductive education is oppressive and denies people with disabilities control of their own lives, Virginia Beardshaw argues exactly the opposite. For her its high expectations and the active learning it fosters gives children control of their lives which they are denied by techniques commonly practised in the UK. Beardshaw also challenges Oliver's attack on practical grounds: Hungary lacks the environmental adaptations that would allow people with disabilities the freedom to move about in wheelchairs. (However, this does not mean that in Britain our built environment is accessible to people in wheelchairs: a trip round most public buildings will reveal this.) If the environment were widely accessible, would this be a reason not to teach children to move independently?

4.18   We have two dramatically contrasting assessments of conductive education. The disagreement between Mike Oliver and Virginia Beardshaw shows some of the ways in which people can reach conflicting conclusions about the value of an educational method. When Will Swann discussed peer tutoring in Unit 6/7, Section 7, he raised some general questions to ask in deciding what teaching methods to adopt. The same questions can usefully be asked about conductive education.

(a)   Compared to what is the method effective? One of Virginia Beardshaw's replies to Mike Oliver is that whatever the shortcomings of conductive education, it is preferable to what was on offer in the UK for her daughter. On the other hand, there are as yet no evaluations of conductive education with other methods of a similar intensity, as Mike Oliver points out.

(b) Would the method be the same method, with the same effects, if it was put into practice in another setting? One of the reasons for establishing the Foundation for Conductive Education in Birmingham was to reproduce the work in Budapest as closely as possible. Andrew Sutton argues that the use of conductive education methods in UK special schools has been very different from Hungarian practice. It remains to be seen, in 1991, if the Birmingham school can reproduce the achievements in Budapest.

(c) Other than the effects on which the claim for effectiveness is based, what other effects might the method have? Mike Oliver objects that conductive education has undesirable effects beyond its professed goals: it devalues the experience and life-styles of people with disabilities.

4.19 At the heart of the debate between Beardshaw and Oliver is a disagreement about goals, not about effectiveness. Disputes about education sometimes turn more on what the goals of teaching should be, rather than on whether these goals have been reached. The success of conductive education in Budapest in reaching its own goals is not a point of contention. Beardshaw and Oliver disagree about whether or not these goals are desirable.

ARGUMENTS ABOUT PREPARATION FOR THE MAINSTREAM

4.20 Now that we have discussed an example of a special curriculum which aims to prepare children for the mainstream, we can widen the discussion to look at the kinds of arguments that are involved in making a case for a special curriculum that is designed with this goal in mind.

Activity 12   Being sceptical about the preparation argument ———

Think of yourself as an arch-sceptic listening to someone else propound the view that some kind of special provision is justified because it will prepare children for a mainstream school or college. What would they have to do to persuade you to accept it? Our ideas follow, but try to work at this yourself. No two arch-sceptics demand quite the same.

4.21 You might want some or all of the following:

(a) *An argument that 'preparation for the mainstream' is a good goal to aim for.*

In arguing that children need to be prepared for the mainstream, we must imply that there are some basic criteria for entry which some children do not meet. In Hungary being able to walk is a condition for admission to school. If this sounds discriminatory to British ears it is probably because this is not an entry requirement widely set in British mainstream schools. But most schools do have such criteria, and sometimes one of them is being able to walk. They are often hidden until put to the test by a child who does not meet them. The developments in learning support and in the mainstream curriculum described in Unit 6/7 were intended to widen the entry criteria to the mainstream for children with learning difficulties. One of the objections to any case for a special curriculum as a preparation for the mainstream is that it does not encourage the mainstream system to be more flexible.

(b) *Evidence that the way to prepare people for the mainstream is by teaching them certain skills, attitudes and abilities before they join it.*

The presence of some children in special education is justified not on the grounds that they are preparing to enter the mainstream curriculum, but rather that they are preparing for mainstream life after school. This is true of many children with severe learning difficulties. The special curriculum that they experience is often said to help them to acquire the skills they will need to participate in ordinary life. This argument rests on the assumption that what stops people from participating in ordinary life is a lack of skill. Yet the experience of many adults with disabilities and learning difficulties is that they are denied participation by others. It is not just that they may lack the personal resources, but that others will not let them use the skills they possess. Attempts by people with learning difficulties to move into ordinary houses are opposed by residents; people with physical disabilities are refused entrance to cinemas because of fire regulations, or they are refused service in pubs. From the point of view of many adults with disabilities, it is not that they need to be prepared for ordinary life, but that ordinary life needs to be prepared for them. This is sometimes presented as an argument against separate special curricula, since, the claim goes, separation denies other people the chance to be prepared for adults with disabilities and learning difficulties. What would persuade you that this argument was correct? Is this an argument against conductive education?

(c) *Evidence that in a mainstream educational environment children are unlikely to learn the skills, attitudes or abilities they need for participation in the mainstream.*

This point needs to be argued case by case. It seems very unlikely that a mainstream environment could provide the intensive teaching offered by conductive education. It is more likely that a mainstream school might contain the resources necessary to teach a blind child to read braille and acquire mobility skills. Whether this is possible depends upon how schools and local authorities organize and distribute their resources. In most cases where preparation for the mainstream is invoked to justify the separation of children, the children concerned do not have physical and sensory disabilities. In Reader 1, Chapter 15, Mel Ainscow, who used to be head of a special school for children described as having moderate learning difficulties, discusses how the school tried to 'accelerate the progress' of its pupils with the aim of returning them successfully to mainstream schools. Preparation here involved teaching children basic skills using 'highly structured' methods. We shall look at these methods in Sections 5 and 6 of this unit.

(d) *Evidence that, in the special educational setting we are concerned with, children are likely to learn the skills they will need to participate in the mainstream.*

The case for conductive education rests in part in the trade-off between the segregation involved and the outcomes. Parents such as Virginia Beardshaw are willing to go to considerable lengths if the teaching really does deliver what it claims. A longstanding criticism of many forms of special provision is that children acquire skills no faster than those who remain in the mainstream. There is a very large body of (largely American) research which has tried to compare the progress made by children in mainstream and special settings. Not surprisingly, the results are diffuse and conflicting since there is so much diversity within special and mainstream settings. So in assessing a claim about preparation for the mainstream, knowledge about the specific circumstances of the claim is important.

(e) *Evidence that moving children to a special environment will not inadvertently prevent the acquisition of other skills, attitudes and abilities that are important to participating in the mainstream.*

In assessing any case for segregation in order to prepare for the mainstream, we need to be specific about what skills will be required when the child joins the mainstream. Vague descriptions of basic skills may not be sufficient. Children who move from a special school into a mainstream school have to cope with a large number of changes to their school lives: the school may be larger and noisier, there may be less personal contact with teachers, teaching approaches may differ, children may be expected to organize their work for themselves to a greater extent, daily routines may be different, there is a new social world to fit into. Coping with these changes is important to survival in a new school. When children move from a special to a mainstream setting, teachers may be only partially aware of the demands on them created by their new peer group and by classroom routines which seem so ordinary that teachers take them for granted. It may turn out that segregation into a special setting makes it harder for children to acquire these skills. They may need a lot of support when they join the mainstream, since it is very difficult to prepare in advance for many of these changes. A carefully planned transition between settings may be important.

SUMMARY

(a) Some special curricula have been defended on the grounds that some children need a period of preparation for the mainstream during which they will acquire the skills they need to take part in the mainstream.

(b) Conductive education is a special curriculum which is seen as a preparation for the mainstream. It aims to teach children with physical disabilities to function independently and adapt to the demands of life without the help of aids. This aim is referred to as 'orthofunction'. As practised in Hungary, it is an intensive full-time programme which emphasizes highly planned active learning in groups, guided by 'conductors', who play the roles of teacher and therapist.

(c) Conductive education has been heavily criticized by some people with disabilities who argue that it devalues their individuality and chosen life-styles, imposes an able-bodied definition of normal life, and distracts attention from the need to change social and physical environments, rather than force people with disabilities to fit into an inflexible environment.

(d) Conductive education has also been defended by other people with disabilities and by parents of children with disabilities on the grounds that it is a significant advance on rehabilitation methods commonly in use in the UK, and involves much higher expectations of what children with physical disabilities can achieve.

(e) In assessing any claim that children need a period of preparation for the mainstream, it is important to ask whether the mainstream could be more flexible so that it does not have restrictive entry criteria; whether effective participation depends on children acquiring skills, attitudes and abilities; whether these skills cannot be learnt in the mainstream; whether these skills will be actually learnt outside the mainstream; and whether the period of preparation will inadvertently make participation in the mainstream more difficult.

5   SEPARATE AND SPECIAL?

5.1   Let's review briefly. We saw in Section 2 how the selection of children into special provision leads to distinctions of treatment and group identities that are not part of the formally planned curriculum. We saw how selection can create separate groups receiving separate curricula which are not always in the interests of the children receiving them. In Section 3, we saw some of the special arrangements which have been made in order to give children access to the mainstream curriculum. In Section 4, we considered ways in which separate special education early on might prepare children for later participation in the mainstream curriculum. But we have not yet tackled the question of whether every child should be seen as a potential participant in some form of mainstream curriculum. Is there a limit to flexibility? In this section we shall look at learners who seem to present the severest tests of the idea of a common curriculum for all.

LEARNING THROUGH TOUCH AND MOVEMENT

5.2   One such group comprises children and young people who have disabilities of both hearing and vision. There are few such children: a DES survey put their numbers in Britain at 800 (Fisher, 1989). SENSE, the national deaf-blind and rubella association, argues that 1,500 is a more realistic figure.

5.3   Often specialist techniques can sound complicated and mysterious, especially when we are only able to read about them instead of observing them in action. The description on pages 60–63 uses photographs of the way deaf-blind children are taught in a unit at Whitefield School, a special school in the London borough of Waltham Forest. We hope it will help you to see how they learn.

SUPPORTING THE EARLIEST STAGES OF LEARNING

5.4   Until 1970 in England and Wales, children with severe and profound learning difficulties were legally excluded from the education system as 'ineducable' (up to 1959), and then as 'unsuitable for education in school'. They attended centres run by local health authorities called junior training centres. As a result of the Education (Handicapped Children) Act (1970) all these children became the responsibility of local education authorities. The transfer to education was made in 1973 in Scotland, but did not happen until 1985 in Northern Ireland.

5.5   Until recently the curriculum in special schools for children with severe and profound learning difficulties has been dominated by the approach known as 'teaching by objectives'. The most important feature of this approach is the insistence that what is to be learnt should be set out in precise, observable and measurable terms. Such teaching objectives are often called 'behavioural objectives', since they specify what the child is to do after the teaching that she could not do before. In schools which rely heavily on this approach large parts of the curriculum consist of activities which are designed to help children to achieve skills set out in detailed lists of objectives arranged in a sequence from least to most complex, or from earlier to later in development.

5.6   The roots of teaching by objectives lie in the theory of learning known as behaviourism, and especially in the work of the American psychologist B. F. Skinner. The central defining feature of behaviourism is the view that human conduct, in all its forms, is no more than behaviour. This includes language, thought, perception, movement and emotion. To explain how people learn is to explain how they come to behave in certain ways. This view is behind the insistence that teaching objectives should be stated in terms of observable behaviour. Behaviourism holds that behaviour changes because of its consequences. According to Skinner, ideas such as 'motives', 'desires' and 'beliefs' do not explain why people do things. This does not mean that people do not have motives, desires and beliefs: Skinner argued that these and other 'mentalisms' are in fact just ways of summarizing tendencies to behave in certain ways; saying that we behave because of motives, desires or beliefs that come before we act does not explain anything. Skinner argued that the causes of behaviour are the consequences of behaviour. After certain consequences we are more likely to repeat the behaviour: such consequences are called 'positive reinforcers'. Other consequences make us less likely to repeat the behaviour, and these 'aversive' events are known as 'punishment'. Most modern behaviourists do not favour the use of punishment as a device in teaching; indeed, many of them have followed Skinner in arguing that schools are places where there are too many aversive consequences and not enough positive reinforcement. The emphasis in behaviourism on positive reinforcement has led to teaching programmes in many special schools, especially those for children with severe learning difficulties, which place great stress on the need to reward children for performing the behaviour specified in the objective. (For an introduction to Skinner's ideas, see Skinner, 1974.)

5.7   The objectives approach involves very tightly planned teaching in which the method and responses required from the child are set out in great detail. The following example is of a boy in a special care unit who was a subject in a research project by Chris Kiernan and his colleagues:

Teaching exploratory play: squeezing

Jonathan was a severely mentally handicapped child who showed very little spontaneous play behaviour. Although he was able to look at objects and reach and grasp, if left on his own with a variety of toys he just sat and sucked his fingers. He handled objects infrequently and with little purpose. At most they were picked up and dropped.

When playing with him it became evident that he did enjoy certain toys, particularly the squeaky animals, although he required his teacher to do the squeezing. Consequently we felt it appropriate to teach him how to do this.

The toys. We selected five different squeaky toys: four animals varying in shape, size and difficulty for squeezing, and a bicycle horn. Two of the animals were easy to grasp, although, as it turned

(continued on p. 64)

Figure 6.

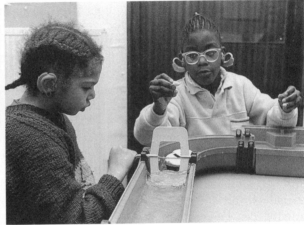

Figure 7.

In Figures 6 and 7, two pupils are playing with a water chute and some boats with their teacher. It is an example of purposeful play which will help them to discover which boats can get through the turning gate and how to control the flow of the water. In Figures 8 and 9, older students are preparing to eat their lunch in their own dining-room, which is in a separate section of the unit from where the younger pupils eat. They help to serve each other and they chat during the meal. Neither of these activities is in any respect untypical of what happens in all schools.

Helping these young people to structure their time is crucial. A frightening experience for young people with minimal hearing or vision is to be constantly surprised by daily events: to lack the anticipation

Figure 8.

Figure 9.

which is part of most people's pattern of living. For children who are given no visual or auditory cues, events can seem unexpected and intrusive. Their fear of change might make them retreat into stereotypical behaviours in order to create their own familiar patterns. In school there is a routine which marks out each period of the day and which distinguishes one day from the next. Staff at the unit help to provide a sequence to the week with a tactile calendar for those children who need it. It is an intensely physical experience, with the children undressed to their underwear. Children feel a contrasting texture each morning. Thus, on Monday they sit at their tables and feel cornflakes; on Tuesday, it is mashed potato; on Wednesday, golden syrup; on Thursday, semolina; on Friday, shaving foam. Staff may help the child to touch the texture, taste it where appropriate and feel it all over their torso. While such means of communication are unfamiliar to most of us, touch and taste become most important where other senses are not operating effectively. It is easy for our inhibitions to prevent us from seeing the potential of these senses. In Figure 10, a boy is feeling golden syrup on his tray, which he then rubs on his torso and face. He enjoys the warm wash afterwards!

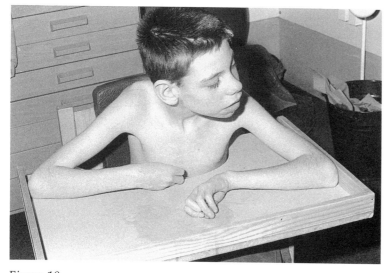

Figure 10.

Another way to help children to understand the pattern of each day is through 'objects of reference'. These are familiar daily objects which they use for a variety of experiences. It might be a basket for shopping, a tray for tactile play, a spoon and cup for dinner and drink time, paper for the toilet, an activity centre for work, jingle bells for auditory training. These objects, which are part of their daily experience, become familiar through their being able to collect them from their own personal shelf and take them to where they will be using them. It is a way of giving ownership of personal experience to that child. Although

Figure 11.

Figure 12.

Figure 13.

it may be staff who help them to play, to eat and to go to the toilet, it is they who take control over those physical objects which are involved. In Figure 11, a very young boy is seen eating his lunch. In Figures 12 and 13 he collects one of his 'objects of reference', a flannel, which he will wash his face with after lunch. This takes place every day but only at the appropriate time, when he has finished a morning snack or his lunch or has been playing with golden syrup. Therefore, it is a task which is not taught in isolation but is directly relevant to what is happening to him now. It gives him some control and helps him make sense of the sequence of his day.

When children can make some sense of what is happening to them, it opens the way for more complex and subtle forms of communication. In Figure 14, a teacher finger-spells words onto a girl's hand. She is able to finger-spell back to him and in this way they can have a meaningful dialogue. She uses a brailler to type out her words, shown in Figure 15.

Figure 14.

Figure 15.

In Figures 16, 17 and 18, we see a young woman who is integrating into a college of further education several days a week. She is talking to her assistant about her morning at college. She uses finger-spelling and BSL. She is now a participant in a mainstream setting.

Figure 16.

Figure 17.

Figure 18.

out, neither was soft enough to use in the first stage of the programme. We planned to teach him to use this range of toys, beginning with the easiest of the animals and ending with the bicycle horn.

Reward. Although we had chosen to teach squeaky toys because Jonathan seemed to like the noise they produced, we provided the additional reward of a crisp for each correct squeeze. It was easy to phase out the reward once he had learned all the necessary skills.

Step 1. We chose a small round policeman as the first toy. In order to produce any noise Jonathan needed to hold him firmly round the middle and squeeze. If he grasped the helmet or feet nothing happened.

During the first session Jonathan was prompted to hold him correctly and squeeze. He was rewarded for each attempt. During the second session we began to fade the prompts, and by the end of that session he was grasping correctly. (It was still necessary to support the policeman while he attempted to grasp. If the policeman fell over Jonathan was unable to stand him upright.) However, he still required the prompt to squeeze him.

This procedure continued for five sessions, with still no attempt at a squeeze from Jonathan. If he was given no prompt he would sit and hold the toy firmly. So we decided to find a much softer squeaky toy which produced a noise at a mere touch. After two prompted attempts at this toy, Jonathan held and squeezed it with ease.

We ran two sessions, sixty attempts, using this easy toy to ensure that the grasping and squeezing were well established. During the following session we tried the policeman three times. We slipped it in between attempts with the easy toy. Jonathan made no attempt to squeeze it although he continued squeezing the other.

Over the next three sessions we introduced the policeman more frequently. Occasionally we left Jonathan holding the policeman, with no reward. On other occasions we prompted him. Towards the end of this third session Jonathan squeezed the policeman once with no prompt. During the following session he squeezed it twice again with no prompt. During the next two sessions there were no successful squeezes. However, in the session after that, the eighth since we had brought back the policeman, he squeezed it six times. This session was made up of seventeen attempts with the policeman, and thirteen with the easy toy.

During the ninth session we used the policeman twenty-seven times and Jonathan produced only one unsuccessful attempt.

Step 2. It had taken eighteen sessions to get Jonathan to squeeze the toy. The aim of step 2 was to fade out the prompt which we gave to the top of the toy while he grasped and squeezed it. During this stage Jonathan developed a new behaviour. Whenever we failed to hold the toy down while he squeezed it, he would either pick it up and shake it or pick it up and suck it. Although these two behaviours appear on our list of exploratory play skills they were not appropriate for the teaching session. Consequently we had to use a combination of prompts and time-out to eliminate them. It took us a further nine sessions to do this.

Step 3. Jonathan was now able to squeeze the toy with no help at all, as long as it was placed upright and in front of him. In order to make the squeezing appropriate in an unsupervised play situation, we had to teach him to pick up the toy when it was on its side.

We now had to reintroduce prompts. These prompts were not to help him grasp and squeeze but to show him how to stand the toy upright. The prompts were faded over eight sessions. By the end of this time Jonathan was able to squeeze the toy without prompt, regardless of how it was given to him.

Step 4. In order to be sure that the squeezing would generalise to play in the classroom and home, we now had to phase out the crisps as a reward. We did this first by requiring him to make two or three successful attempts before he got a crisp. Gradually we required him to do more for each crisp. In addition we began to place the toy at different points on the table. Sometimes he would have to stretch forward to reach it, and at other times he would have to move to his left or right.

The results of the programme. It took us many weeks of work to teach Jonathan to squeeze this toy. However, the programme ensured that he could use this behaviour under most conditions. In order to see whether it generalised to unsupervised play, we observed him playing with a range of toys, including several squeaky animals that he had not seen before. Over a ten-minute period he showed very little finger sucking, a lot of squeezing and squeaking, and several other good exploratory behaviours that we had not taught. Had we finished the programme at the end of step 2 it is unlikely that such good generalisation of the skill would have occurred.

(Kiernan, Jordan and Saunders, 1978, pp. 127–30)

5.8   Jonathan takes a long time to learn to do what is required of him. At step 2, he improvizes by shaking and sucking the toy but, as this was not considered appropriate, this behaviour was eliminated. Through various tactics which prevented Jonathan from playing in this way, the researchers were able to stop him 'doing his own thing' and get him to do what they wanted. Jenny Corbett was teaching Jonathan during the time when he was being used in this research project and could observe both the advantages and disadvantages of this teaching. Jonathan greatly enjoyed the crisps which he was fed for correct responses and he loved being tickled by the researcher. The sessions were a pleasurable experience for him and he went to them with enthusiasm. However, squeezing the toy was of minimal interest to him. It was the researcher and his warm personality which seemed to Jenny to please Jonathan. When he began shaking and sucking the toy instead of squeezing it, this was his way of relating to objects and it could have been viewed as a positive response. Note that the 'prompts' involved squeezing the toy with Jonathan and that it took some time to wean him away from this support. He liked people to play with him rather than be left to play on his own. This programme did extend his skills, but it also negated the particular play activities which he had already developed. They included sucking and shaking objects, exploring his environment in a sensual and unconventional way.

5.9   Was it right to require Jonathan to play in the way defined by the teaching programme? Should Jonathan have been allowed to explore objects in his own ways? Some writers have criticized teaching programmes like Jonathan's on the grounds that children are forced to conform against their will to their teachers' conception of normal activity. Sue Wood and Barbara Shears (1986), two teachers working with children with severe learning difficulties, argued that requiring conformity to such a norm is oppressive and denies children the right to individuality. Compare their view with Mike Oliver's on conductive education:

> Educational practice which aims to normalise children with severe learning difficulties, i.e. make them more normal, devalues them in terms of the people they actually are. It creates handicap itself. Present trends – to use behavioural objectives and teach discrete skills – treat children with severe learning difficulties as objects. Assessment and teaching do not make any significant allowances for children to have perspectives of their own which may differ from the mainstream view about what is desirable and necessary. Within the educational context, children with severe learning difficulties are not seen as children who have minds of their own, but as malfunctioning systems.
>
> (Wood and Shears, 1986, p. 3)

Activity 13   Jess and Brian

How do you react to this argument? To explore it further we shall consider two other examples of children with severe learning difficulties. Read these two short accounts and think about what Wood and Shears' argument would mean in practice for how they should be taught.

Jess

Jess was a girl with no speech who, with Jonathan, was being used as a subject in the same research project. She was the only one among this group who defeated the researcher. He found that the one thing that acted as 'positive reinforcement' was to throw Jess up in the air. As she was heavy, he found this impractical. Jess's parents accepted their daughter as she was and seemed to ignore her limitations. They encouraged her to play the piano maintaining that she was clearly musical. Even when she was an adolescent, they let her play with sand and water, accepted her incontinence, her eating with her hands and her liking for stroking and flicking coloured rags. As the youngest of six children, they treated her as a valued member of the household. Many teachers at the school felt that Jess's parents were quite unrealistic. They dismissed the notion that Jess had a musical ear as a complete fantasy and mere wish-fulfilment. They wanted her parents to co-operate by following behavioural programmes at home that they had started at school, to help Jess learn to take herself to the toilet and to eat with a knife and fork. Her parents resisted, as this control of her behaviour made Jess frustrated and angry.

Brian

Brian disliked being taken to the toilet. He learnt that if he banged his face with his fists when he was being taken to the toilet he would be left alone to wet his pants. Soon his parents gave up the struggle to toilet-train him and left him in nappies. Brian then went on to bang his face when he was asked to do other things he did not like – move out of his favourite chair, have a strange person in the room with him. His life, and the lives of his parents, became more and more restricted.

5.10   One interpretation of Wood and Shears' argument is that the behaviour of children should be accepted as a 'different perspective' on what is desirable. If Jess finds it satisfying to play with sand and water, then she should be allowed to continue to do so. If Brian finds it so hateful to use the toilet that he will injure himself to avoid it, then we should not require him to use it. We should not seek to impose our definitions of normality on these children. In reply we might make a number of points:

(a) This seems to be an argument for not educating certain children at all, for in teaching any child we have in mind that the child will learn things which their teachers think are valuable. To refuse to teach children with severe learning difficulties would be discriminatory – a return perhaps to excluding some children from education.

(b) There are competing interests involved here. Dealing with incontinence is a time-consuming, and for some a distasteful, business. Teaching a child to use the toilet may not be in the immediate interests of the child, but might be justified in the interests of her carers.

(c) People do not like everything that they do. Most of us at some time wish we did not behave in certain ways which we find difficult to avoid. So children's behaviour should not always be taken straightforwardly as personally satisfying.

5.11 In fact, Wood and Shears did not argue that we should give up teaching. Rather, they claimed that teaching should begin from an understanding of children's own view of their world and their own purposes in acting: we should not deny to any child the status of a purposeful human being. Even the most worrying and apparently pointless behaviour can serve a purpose. The key to teaching is to make sense of that purpose and what the child's behaviour means:

> Once it has been accepted that children with severe learning difficulties are individuals with the same basic rights as other people, and therefore the same right to participate in situations in which they are involved, in a self determining manner, other things follow, most notably finding ways of allowing this to happen and being able to recognise when it does – how for example even the most profoundly disabled pupil is an interactive, communicating and self determining person who, given the chance, is quite capable of developing further his own knowledge and understanding.

> (Wood and Shears, 1986, p. 110)

Activity 14 An alternative to objectives

Now read 'Returning to the basics: a curriculum at Harperbury Hospital School' by Dave Hewett and Melanie Nind (Reader 1, Chapter 18). Despite policies aimed at moving people with mental handicaps out of large long-stay hospitals into smaller houses and hostels there are still many residents in mental handicap hospitals. Hospital schools are run, like any other special school, by the local education authority, and attended by hospital residents. The number of children of school age in mental handicap hospitals is now very small indeed, so most hospital schools are attended by adults. In this chapter, Dave Hewett and Melanie Nind explain how the curriculum in their hospital school moved away from the objectives approach towards methods which gave the students a greater role in their own learning. As you read the chapter:

(a) Note down the arguments Hewett and Nind advance against the objectives approach and how their alternative differs from teaching by objectives.

(b) Compare the principles on which Hewett and Nind built their 'intensive interaction' with the arguments for active learning in Unit 6/7.

In the first section of the chapter, Hewett and Nind refer to some of the more common behavioural techniques. Understanding these is not vital to understanding their argument. The techniques they refer to are:

Shaping: This is a method of teaching a new skill by getting the learner to make successive approximations to the target skill. In Jonathan's programme, described earlier, the teacher taught him to squeeze toys by getting him to hold them first and then squeeze them.

Prompting and fading: In Jonathan's programme, the teacher prompted him to produce the desired behaviour. To begin with the prompt might involve lifting his hand and placing it round the toy, later it might be putting his hand on the toy, later again just touching his hand and moving it slightly towards the toy. This process of progressively eliminating the prompt is known as fading.

Chaining: In teaching a skill which is made up of several sequential components, chaining aims to teach one stage at a time. For example, putting on trousers involves getting the trousers into position, pulling them over the legs, doing the zip and buttons up. This skill might be taught by first doing everything for the learner except the last stage, which is the first objective. Once this is mastered, the penultimate stage will be taught, and so on, until the whole skill is acquired. This form of chaining, starting from the last component, is called backward chaining.

Time-out: This is a form of punishment in which the offending learner is put in a quiet area or separate room for a fixed time period, usually a few seconds or minutes. Sometimes time-out does not involve moving the learner, but ignoring him for a very short period.

5.12   What were Hewett and Nind's concerns about their original 'highly structured curriculum'?

(a) It promoted authoritarian relationships between teachers and learners which did not help learning. The effectiveness of behavioural programmes is usually assessed in terms of the success with which children achieve the set objectives. Some children, like Jonathan, can, in time, be taught to perform as required. But the child's performance is not the only effect of the teaching. Teaching usually has several simultaneous consequences. As well as learning a skill, children engaged in a tightly defined behavioural programme are also participating in a social relationship which places them and their teacher in certain roles. Sue Wood and Barbara Shears argue that there is a fundamental contradiction between behavioural programmes which aim to teach children the skills they will need to be independent, and the relationships established by the teaching, which require children to be dependent:

> Our argument is that teacher–pupil relations, in the education of children with severe learning difficulties, are dominated by relations of imposition, where these children are required to learn in a prescribed way, without regard to their views or desires, and narrowing their options within situations to such an extent they have no viable alternative to compliance … such relations of teaching amplify the role of children with severe learning difficulties as dependent people.
> (Wood and Shears, 1986, p. 60)

(b) Teaching programmes based on the objectives approach start with a definition of the teaching problem to be solved: it is a skill deficit. So the solution is to teach skills. But Hewett and Nind's analysis takes us further. Their students certainly do lack skills, but skills learned in isolation from a purpose that the learners wish to achieve are of limited value to them. It is not helpful to be taught a skill for which you can see no use. 'Intensive interaction' involves helping learners to adopt purposes for themselves and to achieve their own goals in interactions.

(c) The curriculum left little room to respond to differences in individual interests and strengths. One of the consequences of a curriculum made up of skill checklists, strictly applied, is that learners are understood in terms of those skills. It is difficult to take into account anything that is not part of the checklist, even though it may be educationally relevant. (Compare this with the discussion of statements of attainment in Reader 1, Chapter 7.) Here the way the skill checklist is used is important: A skill checklist can be anything from a useful guide to what to look for, to the whole curriculum.

5.13   In Unit 6/7 we saw a number of arguments for pupils being actively involved in their own learning:

- it enables children to bring their existing knowledge to bear, and relate what they already know to what they are learning;

- it helps the teacher to see what the pupil knows and understands;

- it enables children to develop a commitment to their own learning;

- it helps children to make their own thinking explicit.

5.14   In 'intensive interaction' teaching students are actively engaged. Teachers try to respond sensitively to their purposes and actions; students are involved in defining their own curriculum, and are able to exert control over their environment. But the way in which these principles are realized in practice, and the activity in which the students engage, are radically different from the examples we saw in Unit 6/7. Hewett and Nind list a number of benefits for their students: greater enjoyment; a reduction in violent and negative behaviour; greater sociability; and more awareness of their immediate environment.

WORKING TOWARDS LEVEL 1?

5.15   However they are taught, the learners that Hewett and Nind are concerned with seem to need a curriculum that is very different from the mainstream curriculum in most schools. Yet they were included in the groups entitled, according to the NCC, to 'a broad and balanced curriculum, including the National Curriculum'. The advent of the

National Curriculum forced teachers in special schools to look more carefully at just how much of their curricula could and should be the same as those of mainstream schools. Doubts about the capacity of the National Curriculum to include all children without modification were evident from the time it was first mooted in 1987. It was these doubts and concerns that led the government to introduce the statutory exemptions referred to in Unit 1/2 (paras 2.24 and 3.62).

Activity 16   A National Curriculum for Patricia and Stelios ⎯⎯⎯

Patricia and Stelios, described by Dave Hewett and Melanie Nind (in Reader 1, Chapter 18), are adults whose learning does not seem to fit the National Curriculum very well. Look again at the descriptions of their learning in 'Describing our practice'. How might we describe their learning in National Curriculum terms? If you are familiar with the details of the National Curriculum, what parts of it might apply to them?

⎯⎯⎯⎯⎯⎯⎯⎯⎯⎯⎯⎯⎯⎯⎯⎯⎯⎯⎯⎯⎯⎯⎯⎯⎯⎯⎯⎯⎯⎯⎯⎯⎯

5.16   One solution to the problems created by the National Curriculum for learners with multiple and profound disabilities is to exempt them altogether. But this carries some unhappy implications. Does it mean that such children are a completely different educational species? Partly to avoid such implications, the idea of 'Working towards Level 1' (sometimes 'Working within Level 1') was invented, and promoted through official bodies such as the NCC. Working towards Level 1 involves loose interpretations of Level 1 statements of attainment, so that activities that subject working parties almost certainly did not envisage are defined as part of Level 1. Judy Sebba led the National Curriculum Development Team for pupils with severe learning difficulties. She has described how history might be used with children with severe learning difficulties. In key stage 1, history includes a study of the conventions of time, pupils' own histories and events in their lives. This might mean pupils learning to appreciate the sequence of daily and weekly school routines. As history, within the National Curriculum, is seen as helping to give pupils a sense of identity, Sebba suggested that:

> In all the strategies which teachers adopt to heighten their pupils' perceptions of their individual identities, they can remind themselves that not only are they attempting something which has always been a pre-eminent aim of the personal and social curriculum, but also that they are working within the framework of National Curriculum History.
>
> (Sebba and Clarke, 1991, pp. 121–2)

5.17   Working towards Level 1 was a subject of growing concern and criticism as the problems it created began to emerge. It produced some astonishing linguistic contortions. The staff of one special school were dismayed by an example they received in advisory documents:

How can the following be justified?

'A child who shows awareness of having a dirty nappy can be said to be working towards Science Attainment Target 5: Human influences on the Earth (Level 1: know that human activities produce a wide range of waste products. Level 2: know that some waste products decay naturally).'

(Tye Green School staff, 1991, p. 13)

Does the unfortunate child have to be left for several days with nappy unchanged in order to achieve Level 2?

5.18   Working towards Level 1 has also been criticized as the antithesis of responding to the needs of individual children. The staff of Tye Green School called this, 'the unacceptable practice of fitting the child into a curriculum instead of designing the curriculum for the child'. The National Curriculum was never designed with children with severe learning difficulties in mind, and so why should it now form the basis for their education? Bernard Emblem and Gina Conti-Ramsden (1990) argued that working towards Level 1 treats many children as long-term failures:

> Those who fall before the first level are failures before they begin. What hope for those, then, who have no prospect of reaching Level 1 and whose annual reviews speak of working towards Level 1 for a decade or more, challenging the fundamental educational tenet of teaching to success?

(Emblem and Conti-Ramsden, 1990, p. 90)

In these circumstances what looks like an entitlement may turn out to be nothing of the sort. Brahm Norwich cautions that: 'entitlements can be double edged, particularly if the entitlement is to something which is not relevant to the needs of particular children. In such cases entitlements can turn into rigid impositions' (Norwich, 1990, pp. 159–60).

WORKING TOWARDS THE MAINSTREAM

5.19   Can we think of the learners we have discussed in this section as having a place in the mainstream curriculum? The great majority of children with severe and profound learning difficulties are in special schools, but not everywhere. Springfield Road Junior School, Derbyshire, is a school whose pupils cover an enormously wide range of attainments. Up to 1982 Springfield Road was effectively three separate institutions on the same site: the mainstream school, an 'MLD unit' and an 'SLD unit'. The latter contained a special care group of children with profound and multiple disabilities. A new head appointed in 1982, Ian Mitchell, took the opportunity to begin to bring these groups closer together, having concluded that their separation led to bad consequences:

The way pupils were labelled not only exposed them to a totally different curriculum but, worse, a different set of adult expectations. I began to believe that these expectations influenced the behaviour and performance of the children.

(Mitchell quoted in O'Grady, 1990, p. 3)

5.20   At Springfield Road children are now mainly taught in what Ian Mitchell calls 'all ability groups' with extensive staff support. By merging the staff resources of the three institutions, the school was able to reduce class sizes to between fourteen and eighteen. With fourteen teachers and fourteen educational care officers between 230 children, staffing levels can be matched flexibly to learning needs. Teachers at Springfield Road have found that they have been able to include very diverse groups in common experiences by diversifying lessons in ways we discussed in Unit 6/7. Here is an example:

The use of variety in teaching strategies was illustrated in a lesson about air pressure. The teacher used plastic syringes to illustrate the principle to the mixed ability group of eight and nine-year-olds. Two syringes were linked with a piece of plastic tubing and when the plunger of one was pushed in, the plunger of the other came out. Before this demonstration the children made models of Humpty Dumpty from paper and plastic bottles.

The climax of the lesson came when the Humpty Dumpty models were placed on a cardboard wall to be pushed off by the plunger. Each time they fell the class sang Humpty Dumpty. The song was probably the most important moment for Emma, who has learning difficulties. It was a time she could fully share with her class and an opportunity to improve her language abilities. For other pupils the sophisticated demonstration of a scientific principle provided the main lesson. What mattered in this class was not that all children learned the same thing at the same time, but that everybody benefitted in their own way.

(O'Grady, 1990, p. 4)

5.21   Springfield Road contains a group called the 'early learning group'. This consists of children with profound and multiple disabilities aged up to nineteen, and children who are there for a short period being assessed before final placement. It includes children who would typically be in the special care unit in a special school.

The unit is a colourful, lively place in the centre of the school and has many visitors. One room is a 'Snoezelen' multi-sensory room which stimulates children by sound, a variety of patterns and pictures and things to touch. The children go out to assembly, and perhaps to lunch and other all-school activities. Many attend classes in the rest of the school on a part-time basis and will eventually be integrated full-time.

(O'Grady, 1990, pp. 5–6)

Springfield Road Junior School: one of the few 'all-ability' schools in the UK (photos courtesy John Rutter).

5.22 Springfield Road is a school that has begun to explore ways in which, for some of the time, children with profound learning difficulties can share a common curriculum with the rest of the school. This does not mean forcing them to conform to an inappropriate set of demands, but rather searching for appropriate learning opportunities within a flexible mainstream curriculum. The presence of the 'early learning group' in the school makes this exploration possible, whilst at the same time providing the resources for special experiences for these learners. In Unit 16, we shall investigate how a mainstream secondary school responds to the inclusion of a group of children with profound learning difficulties, and look more systematically at the idea of a school for all, where 'all' really means 'all'.

SUMMARY

(a) Children who have particularly severe disabilities seem to challenge our capacity to include all children within a common curriculum. Children who are deaf and blind are one such group who need many learning experiences over a long period that are not part of most schools' mainstream curriculum.

(b) The curriculum for children with severe and profound learning difficulties in special schools has been dominated by the objectives approach, which involves the detailed specification of teaching goals and highly controlled teaching methods.

(c) The objectives approach has been popular because of its evident success in teaching new behaviours to children excluded from education until 1970 in England and Wales. However, it has been criticized as promoting dependence and passivity in learners, as failing to recognize their individuality, and as teaching skills in isolation from purposes.

(d) 'Intensive interaction' is an alternative approach to the curriculum for learners with profound disabilities, concerned with the development of preverbal communication. It is based on the principles that teaching should respond to the learner's initiatives and purposes, and that patterns of interaction and activity should be negotiated between teacher and learner.

(e) The National Curriculum has created dilemmas for teachers working with children with severe and profound learning difficulties who have had to consider how their curricula might be said to be part of Level 1. This has raised doubts about whether the National Curriculum is in fact a common educational entitlement.

(f) Children with profound learning difficulties have been included in some mainstream schools, and have been able to benefit from some aspects of mainstream school life, whilst at the same time gaining access to experiences appropriate to them, but not to all learners.

6 FROM SPECIAL TO MAINSTREAM

6.1   When someone says that a child 'needs' special educational provision, it is seldom a claim with the solidity of statements like 'people need food' or 'you need a racket to play tennis'. The assertion that a child needs a special curriculum, or special arrangements in school, depends on a view of what is appropriate for that child's education, and this is something that is subject to disagreement. None of the varieties of special treatment that we have discussed are uncontentious. Advocates of conductive education would prefer children to be able to speak and write without technological support. Advocates of a bilingual approach to the education of deaf children dispute the rationale of natural auralism. The objectives approach, for so long the mainstay of the education of children with profound learning difficulties, is now criticized for a number of reasons.

6.2   The need to respond to differences between learners in the experiences we provide for them at school is not so contentious. How we do so is. The final reading for this unit is one person's account of his changing stance on how the education system should respond to the diversity of learners.

Activity 16   Changing track

Now read 'Becoming a reflective teacher' by Mel Ainscow (Reader 1, Chapter 15). Mel Ainscow has been an influential figure in special education since the 1970s. His book with David Tweddle, *Preventing Learning Failure* (Ainscow and Tweddle, 1979), played an important role in encouraging special schools for children with learning difficulties to adopt the objectives approach. In the second section of the chapter, he describes the work of the special school where he was head. This will give you a clearer picture of how the objectives curriculum has been applied in a school for children designated as having moderate learning difficulties. Ainscow also lists the limitations he now sees in the approach. In the third section, Ainscow describes how, as a local authority adviser, he established a staff development programme which amongst other things encouraged teachers in ordinary schools to use the objectives approach for children experiencing difficulties in learning. Then in the fourth section, Ainscow describes how he came to question responses to diversity which involved the creation of separate, special curricula. As you read, note down:

(a) the reasons Ainscow gives for the choice of the objectives approach, the arguments against the approach, and your reactions to them;

(b) Ainscow's arguments for responding to diversity through the development of the mainstream curriculum.

You will find he makes several points that we have already taken up here and in Unit 6/7.

6.3   Ainscow mentions three reasons for the choice of the objectives approach in his special school:

(a)   A wish to compensate for what the staff saw as the paucity of their pupils' experiences. Compare this with the discussion of language deprivation theory in Unit 6/7 Section 5.

(b)   A general criticism of the quality of special education and the inadequacy of the curriculum. Note that these concerns continued throughout the 1980s, as we discussed in Section 2.

(c)   The influence of behaviourist psychology. The links between an educational practice and its underlying theory are always complex and indirect. Not all behaviourists agree that the objectives approach is a valid application of the theory. Kevin Wheldall and Ted Glynn (1989) are two behaviourists who are now critical of teaching by objectives:

> In the past, some behavioural psychologists believed that skills and bodies of knowledge could, and should, be broken down into a series of so-called behavioural objectives which when appropriately sequenced and taught to mastery level would guarantee effective learning. The idea was that the steps would be so small that errorless learning would be possible. This ignores the fact that errors, properly responded to, can be very powerful learning opportunities …

> In British educational psychology the enthusiastic application of behavioural objectives to curriculum design has led to the neglect of the child's behaviour as exerting an influence on the teacher's behaviour. Such a curriculum becomes both 'teacher-proof' and 'child-proof', an achievement which some psychologists seemed to be proud of! Living, interacting human beings become an irritating intrusion into a perfect system. The system and the curriculum are then in danger of becoming fixed, being seen as the only way to learn, the only path for all children to follow. But we know that learning in the world outside the classroom is not like this. Individuals learn similar skills and concepts and master similar areas of knowledge by very different routes and processes. There is no one yellow brick road to success.

> (Wheldall and Glynn, 1989, p. 21)

6.4   Mel Ainscow's reservations about the objectives approach go beyond the details of the teaching methods. He argues that the approach fostered segregation, and made mainstream teachers feel inadequate. These are not so much criticisms of the objectives approach; they concern separate special provision in general. Ainscow argues that special provision encourages people to attribute problems in schools to children rather than to schools, teachers and curricula, that segregation has bad effects on the attitudes and expectations of pupils, teachers and parents and discourages mainstream teachers from taking responsibility for all children. By now these will be familiar arguments to you. Ainscow's wish is not that we should give up the objectives approach, but that we should 'give up the search for special teaching methods for special children'. But objectives still seem to have an important place in Ainscow's new approach, since 'Are objectives being achieved?' is one of his four key questions. It is difficult to know what this means in practice. It might be possible, though sometimes awkward, to describe teaching of the kind we saw in TV3, *Rich Mathematical Activities*, and TV4, *The Write to Choose*, as having objectives. If so, then they are very different from the objectives which were set for children in Ainscow's special school.

6.5   Ainscow's own alternative to the search for special methods is not precisely defined, although he does set out some broad goals and processes by which he thinks schools can improve on what they do. He wants schools to become more effective for all their children, 'attempting to provide forms of teaching that take account of the individual needs of all children', and he advocates co-operative group work, peer coaching, pupil choice and negotiated records of achievement (a form of continuous assessment of individual progress). In assessing whether or not a school has improved we must have some notion of what good practice is, and what would be better than what the school is currently doing. The fact that a school is busy solving problems co-operatively and that its teachers are all being reflective practitioners does not necessarily mean that it is improving (although openness to new ideas is usually a useful quality). It may be trying to solve the wrong problems, or coming up with solutions that make things worse. Its teachers' reflections may lead them to choose worse methods than hitherto. We do not need to agree on what counts as good practice to see this. So while a school which is a problem-solving organization might be better placed to improve itself, something more is needed: a theory of good practice.

6.6   Ainscow does not say how far he would take his argument that we should give up the search for special teaching methods and concentrate on developing curricula which respond to the needs of all children. He has moved to a position where he no longer believes that there should be selection for children who find their way into 'MLD' special schools. Nor does he say how he would fit into this picture the demands of children with physical and sensory disabilities. In the last four units we have explored ways in which mainstream curricula might respond to the attainments, interests and disabilities of a great many of the learners who are typically seen as having special educational needs. We have also seen how some children are selected for educational experiences that are distinct from mainstream curricula, and we have discussed some of the consequences of selection. How far would you take the quest for a non-selective curriculum?

7 INVESTIGATIONS

Views on selection

7.1   In this option you investigate the views of a small group of three or four teachers on selection and grouping. Your approach will need to take into account the settings in which they work, since the forms of selection they will be familiar with will depend on whether they have worked in primary, secondary or special schools. The aim is to explore the kinds of selection and grouping favoured, and the reasons for these choices. Each interview should last no more than 30 minutes. You should ask your interviewees:

(a) to give basic details of the job they do;

(b) to describe the way the groups they currently teach are selected (in secondary schools this may be quite complex);

(c) to discuss the strengths and drawbacks of the selection methods currently in use in their school, and to compare them with other methods they have experience of;

(d) to describe changes they would like to see in the way groups are formed in their current school;

(e) to consider the implications for them of a move to more heterogeneous groupings of learners.

Access to the curriculum for individual learners

7.2   You may know of a pupil in a mainstream or a special school who has a disability that calls for individual arrangments to be made to give them access to the curriculum. In this option you investigate what curricular adaptations and supports have been provided for one pupil with a physical or sensory disability. You should find out:

(a) what supports and adaptations are available to the pupil, in the form of staffing, adaptations to teaching methods and materials, adaptations to timetables, technology, etc.

(b) how these supports and adaptations have developed in the past few years;

(c) the limitations of the current arrangements and views on how they could be improved.

You may need to talk to teachers, parents and the pupil concerned to have a range of perspectives. A short period of observation (one lesson at the most) may also be useful in some cases.

The impact of the National Curriculum

7.3   Has the National Curriculum established a common entitlement for all pupils, or has it increased distinctions in the school experience of different groups of pupils? In this option you investigate this question by talking to a small group of three or four teachers. They might be learning support teachers, or class/subject teachers in mainstream or special schools. They need not be from the same school, indeed comparison between teachers in different schools will be useful. Each interview should last no more than 30 minutes. You should ask your interviewees:

(a) to give basic details of their job;

(b) to describe the changes in their own practice which they believe have resulted from the National Curriculum;

(c) to give their views on the impact of the National Curriculum on children who experience learning difficulties or have disabilities.

REFERENCES

ABRAMS, D., JACKSON, D. and ST CLAIRE, L. (1990) 'Social identity and the handicapping functions of stereotypes: children's understanding of mental and physical handicap', *Human Relations*, **43**, pp. 1085–98.

AINSCOW, M. and TWEDDLE, D. (1979) *Preventing Classroom Failure*, Chichester, John Wiley.

ALLEN, J., COCKERILL, H., DAVIES, E., FULLER, P., JOLLEFF, N., LARCHER, J., NELMS, G. and WINYARD. S. (1989) *Augmentative Communication: more than just words*, Oxford, ACE Centre.

BALL, S. J. (1981) *Beachside Comprehensive: a case study of secondary schooling*, Cambridge, Cambridge University Press.

BOOTH, T. (1988) 'Challenging conceptions of integration' in BARTON, L. (ed.) *The Politics of Special Educational Needs*, London, Falmer Press.

BRENNAN, M. (1987) 'British Sign Language: the language of the deaf community', in BOOTH, T. and SWANN, W. (eds) *Including Pupils with Disabilities*, Milton Keynes, Open University Press/The Open University.

BYERS, R. (1990) 'Topics: from myths to objectives', *British Journal of Special Education*, **17**, pp. 109–12.

CALL CENTRE (1991) *Microtechnology and Disabled Learners: an interactive training and information resource*, Edinburgh, CALL Centre.

CROPP, D. (1987) 'The B6 incident: pupil perceptions of integration', in BOOTH, T. and SWANN, W. (eds) *Including Pupils with Disabilities*, Milton Keynes, Open University Press/The Open University.

DEPARTMENT OF EDUCATION AND SCIENCE (DES) (1978) *Special Educational Needs*, London, HMSO (the Warnock Report).

DEPARTMENT OF EDUCATION AND SCIENCE (DES) (1989a) *Report by HM Inspectors on Educating Physically Disabled Pupils*, London, DES.

DEPARTMENT OF EDUCATION AND SCIENCE (DES) (1989b) *Report by HM Inspectors on a Survey of Pupils with Emotional/Behavioural Difficulties in Maintained Special Schools and Units*, London, DES.

EMBLEM, B. and CONTI-RAMSDEN, G. (1990) 'Towards Level 1: reality or illusion?', *British Journal of Special Education*, **17**, pp. 88–90.

EVANS, P. and WARE, J. (1987) *'Special Care' Provision: the education of children with profound and multiple learning difficulties*, Windsor, NFER-Nelson.

FISHER, A. (1989) 'Making sense without sight or sound', *The Times Educational Supplement*, 18 August 1989, p. 7.

FURNHAM, A. and GIBBS, M. (1984) 'School children's attitudes towards the handicapped', *Journal of Adolescence*, **7**, pp. 99–118.

GALLOWAY, D. (1985) *Schools, Pupils and Special Educational Needs,* London, Croom Helm.

GAMBLE, J. and PALMER, J. (1989) 'The adjustment class as an integrating part of the main school' in BELL, G. H. and COLBECK, B. (eds) *Experiencing Integration: The Sunnyside Action Inquiry Project,* London, Falmer Press.

GOTTLIEB, J. (1975) 'Public, peer and professional attitudes towards mentally retarded persons' in BEGAB, M. J. and RICHARDSON, S. A. (eds) *The Mentally Retarded and Society: a social science perspective,* Baltimore, University Park Press.

GREGORY, S. and BISHOP, J. (1988) 'The mainstreaming of primary age deaf children in the United Kingdom', paper presented to the International Symposium on Hearing Impaired Pupils in Regular Schools, Berlin.

HARGREAVES, D. (1967) *Social Relations in a Secondary School,* London, Routledge and Kegan Paul.

HARRISON, D. E. (1986) 'The education of hearing-impaired children in local ordinary schools – a survey', *Journal of the British Association of Teachers of the Deaf,* **10**, pp. 96–102.

HEWSTONE, M. and BROWN, R. (1986) *Contact and Conflict in Intergroup Encounters,* Oxford, Basil Blackwell.

HOGG, M. A. and ABRAMS, D. (1988) *Social Identifications: a social psychology of intergroup relations and group processes,* London, Routledge.

INCE, S., JOHNSTONE, H. and SWANN, W. (1985) *Breaking Down the Barriers: the history of an integration project,* unpublished report.

KIERNAN, C., JORDAN, R. and SAUNDERS, C. (1978) *Starting Off: establishing play and communication in the handicapped child,* London, Souvenir Press.

KYLE, J. and WOLL, B. (1985) *Sign Language: the study of deaf people and their language,* Cambridge, Cambridge University Press.

LACEY, C. (1970) *Hightown Grammar,* Manchester, Manchester University Press.

LAMBERT, M. (1989) 'The Birmingham Institute: the daily routine', *The Conductor,* **2**(5), pp. 14–15.

LAMBERT, M. (1990) 'Conductive education and the Birmingham Institute: collaboration in training across the East/West divide', paper presented to the International Special Education Congress, Cardiff.

LANE, H. (1984) *When the Mind Hears,* New York, Random House.

NATIONAL CURRICULUM COUNCIL (NCC) (1989) *A Curriculum for All,* York, NCC.

NORWICH, B. (1990) *Reappraising Special Needs Education,* London, Cassell.

O'GRADY, C. (1990) *Integration Working,* London, Centre for Studies on Integration in Education.

POWELL, C. (1989) 'Speaking up for auralism', *Special Children,* **27**, pp. 10–12.

PREDDY, D. and MITTLER, P. (1981) *Children with Severe Learning Difficulties: a survey in North-West England,* Final Report to the Department of Education and Science (Grant No. P 62/21/01).

SEBBA, J. and CLARKE, J. (1990) 'Meeting the needs of pupils in history and geography' in ASHDOWN, R., CARPENTER, B. and BOVAIR, K. (eds) *The Curriculum Challenge: access to the National Curriculum for pupils with learning difficulties,* London, Falmer Press.

SKINNER, B. F. (1974) *About Behaviourism,* London, Jonathan Cape.

SPENCER, S. and ROSS, M. (1989) 'Closing the gap', *Special Children,* **28**, pp. 20–1.

SWANN, W. (1987a) 'Being with Sam: four children talk about their classmate' in BOOTH, T. and SWANN, W. (eds) *Including Pupils with Disabilities,* Milton Keynes, Open University Press/The Open University.

SWANN, W. (1987b) 'Support for Mark: the learning experience of a six-year-old with partial sight' in BOOTH, T., POTTS, P. and SWANN, W. (eds) *Preventing Difficulties in Learning,* Oxford, Basil Blackwell/The Open University.

TAYLOR, G. (1989) 'The Birmingham Institute', *The Conductor,* **2**(5), p. 15.

TYE GREEN SCHOOL STAFF (1991) 'Broad, balanced … and relevant?', *Special Children,* **44**, pp. 11–13.

WATSON, J. and VINCENT, T. (1987) 'Microcomputing and the education of children with visual disabilities in ordinary schools' in BOOTH, T. and SWANN, W. (eds) *Including Pupils with Disabilities,* Milton Keynes, Open University Press/The Open University.

WELSH OFFICE (1983) *A Whole Community: the education of educationally sub-normal (severe) children in Wales,* HMI Occasional Paper, Cardiff, Welsh Office.

WHELDALL, K. and GLYNN, T. (1989) *Effective Classroom Learning,* Oxford, Basil Blackwell.

WOOD, D., WOOD, H., GRIFFITHS, A. and HOWARTH, I. (1986) *Teaching and Talking with Deaf Children,* Chichester, John Wiley.

WOOD, S. and SHEARS, B. (1986) *Teaching Children with Severe Learning Difficulties: a radical reappraisal,* Beckenham, Croom Helm.

ACKNOWLEDGEMENTS

Grateful acknowledgement is made to the following for permission to reproduce material in this unit:

Text

Wright, A. (1989) 'Faces of despair' in Allen, J. *et al.* (eds) *Augmentative Communication: more than just words*, Oxford, ACE Centre; Kiernan, C., Jordan, R. and Saunders, C. (1978) *Starting Off: establishing play and communication in the handicapped child*, Sourvenir Press, © 1978 Chris Kiernan, Rita Jordan and Chris Saunders; extract from the BBC2 programme *One in Four*, 14 February 1990, courtesy of the BBC, Chris Davies and Angela Smith.

Illustrations

page 27: CALL Centre (1991) *Microtechnology and Disabled Learners: an interactive training and information resource*, CALL Centre, University of Edinburgh; *page 30*: courtesy of the Blissymbols Communication Resource Centre; *page 33 (top)*: Sunderland Echo, (*bottom left and right*): ACE Centre, Ormerod School, Oxford; *page 42*: from illustrations by Martin Connell and Linda Hurd in Brennan, M. 'British Sign Language: the language of the Deaf community' in Booth, T. and Swann, W. (eds) (1987) *Including Pupils with Disabilities*, Milton Keynes, Open University Press/The Open University; *page 48*: Foundation for Conductive Education/Richard Smith; *page 74*: courtesy John Rutter.

E242: UNIT TITLES

Unit 1/2   Making Connections

Unit 3/4   Learning from Experience

Unit 5   Right from the Start

Unit 6/7   Classroom Diversity

Unit 8/9   Difference and Distinction

Unit 10   Critical Reading

Unit 11/12   Happy Memories

Unit 13   Further and Higher

Unit 14   Power in the System

Unit 15   Local Authority?

Unit 16   Learning for All